Universities Between Two Worlds

Universities
Between
Two Worlds

W. Roy Niblett

 University of London Press Ltd

ISBN 0 340 17963 5
Copyright © 1974 W. R. Niblett

University of London Press Ltd
St Paul's House, Warwick Lane, London EC4P 4AH

Printed in Great Britain by
T. & A. Constable Ltd
Hopetoun Street, Edinburgh EH7 4NF

Contents

Preface

No implication is intended in the title that the universities are in separate case from other institutions of higher education: all are 'between two worlds'. All, that is, are inescapably faced with questions about their function at a time when men are in course of losing faith in (i) a faster and faster pursuit of economic prosperity as a self-sufficient end; (ii) the principle of 'my country right or wrong'; and (iii) the authority of imposed dogma.

It may be one hundred years—or hundreds—before all the consequences of these psychic shifts are seen. In the meantime higher education will, and must, continue to develop. It must do so, if for no other reason, because of the need to produce the experts of a thousand kinds required to keep things running; and with new complexities rearing their hydra heads, these experts will become more and more indispensable—in, for example, food production, town planning, transport, medicine, law, management.

By itself such development supplies no answer to problems of why? rather than how? But 'why?' questions face intelligent men and women whether they are in colleges of liberal arts or technology, in polytechnics or universities. They can evade them by concentrating on the immediate, the useful, the practical. That is in a curious way a form of unworldliness. In the long run, however, such a retreat breeds discontent, a split in the self, a profound dis-ease.

Yet to say even now that men, or universities, not merely are 'between two worlds' but that one world is dead and 'the other powerless to be born' is an exaggeration. Men still retain many certainties. They dare not do anything else. But the hold is precarious. Much will depend upon whether people can be boldly educated in self knowledge, in facing all the facts, in capacity for experience, imagination, humanity, religious sense. Otherwise they will have to stay in a world whose credibility is threatened by the meaningless plethora of material goods it goes on producing. They will have to forget whatever they don't want to remember. And that is another name for de-humanisation.

Universities have an enormous responsibility to give their students an education that will awaken men, putting them into touch with truth at every level, the source of the power to bring a world to birth.

The content both of this volume and of several of those which will follow it in this series owes a good deal to discussions in colloquia and working parties of which I was chairman. Their meetings were facilitated by a grant, gratefully received, from the Joseph Rowntree Charitable Trust. The names of members of the working parties are listed in an appendix. To four of them—Marjorie Reeves, James Robertson, Frances Stevens and George Whitfield—I owe a special and personal debt: they read the manuscript of the book and made many helpful suggestions in the hope that it might be improved. But what it says is entirely my responsibility; neither they nor other members of the working parties will necessarily agree with all, or even most, of it.

My debt is also considerable to many friends in the U.S., to the Center for the Study of Democratic Institutions in Santa Barbara at which Chapter 5 was presented in an earlier version as a paper and to the *Times Higher Education Supplement* which has allowed me to reproduce several paragraphs which I originally wrote for its pages.

Susan Rawlings has typed and re-typed the manuscript with the combination of superb efficiency and patience I have come to rely on from her. Rosalind Greenbaum and Mary Howarth have also given valuable help in its preparation.

I owe most, however, to my wife without whose constant support and wise—sometimes chastening—advice neither this book nor the series to follow would have seen the light of day.

Chapter 1

Introduction: Universities Under Attack

Until recently universities were not in doubt of their own authority. A combination of causes is now disturbing that state of mind. The rapid expansion in provision of higher education in institutions other than universities is one cause; another is our uncertainty about the state of knowledge itself—the simple days are past when 'objective study' was expected to yield solutions to most of our problems. A third cause is our present lack of confidence about goals, both social and personal, and our almost unconscious readiness to substitute for them a number of technical achievements which, though impressive, consumer-oriented and necessary, are far more easily come by.

A great many books, some very wise, have been written in the last twenty years on policies and planning in higher education. The subject is one of vital concern to the future both of the leading countries of the world and of those which follow: a system of higher education anywhere is a major investment, and its development not to be undertaken unadvisedly, lightly or wantonly. People are certainly beginning to recognise, and to say, that higher education needs to become a great deal more responsible to society and to its own students than it has been, at any rate in the recent past. But being responsible to society cannot simply mean doing what the public happens at the moment to think should be done. Nor can one assume that the achievement of social goals and of personal development will never conflict. Universities are far from realising the extent of the change of outlook that is required of them: changes of assumption, changes of orientation, changes in the content of what they teach. The pressure on universities in recent years to expand has been tremendous but it has not yet caused them to think in any fundamental way about their new function in society. They have been too content to go on producing technically educated people in separate fields, for a society neither very sure nor very thoughtful about where it is going.

But the products of our institutions of higher education need more and more to be both effective as professionals and capable of personal insights into what is more important and what is less so. We certainly do not want an élite segregated in a very few university institutions; rather we want every man to carry his own éliteness within him.

How is that, or anything like it, to be brought about? In fact, the pressure grows on higher education in almost every country to produce graduates useful to a society eager for more and more technology and know-how. This pressure can be seen to have been growing for at least a hundred years. Newman's idea of the Oxford type of university—educating gentlemen and educating them one by one—and Fichte's and Humboldt's ideas of the Berlin type of university, educating those dedicated to adding by research to knowledge for its own sake, have both for some time been dated concepts. Their viability depended upon the existence of a demand for gentlemen, or for leaders of church, state and empire, or for men of pure knowledge, who could give their judgements from outside the battle—with detachment, confidence and maybe wisdom for others to apply. The demand for people of any of these sorts has notably lessened in a world grown democratic, in which colonialism is suspect and advice is sought most from those who are seen both to have knowledge and to be able to apply it usefully. Institutions of higher education in most of the dominant countries have been supported by industry and the state to produce people likely to help their country's prosperity and welfare in particular ways—as agriculturalists, economists, administrators or experts in a hundred other fields.

What, then, are universities for today? To be useful and obedient at the behest of society? They are between two worlds—one not as yet fully born.

In the past twenty five years, however, there has been discernible, in a wide scatter of countries, a movement which cannot be explained in utilitarian terms. The astonishingly powerful currents making for the acceptance of comprehensive schools; sweeping public opinion towards the creation of 'universities without walls', not chiefly orientated to the study of technologies; the growing acceptance of the idea of life-long education, do not really make sense if utility is the main criterion. The most ardent and honest defenders of comprehensive principles indeed rarely defend them on such a ground —but rather on grounds of fairness, justice, the rights of citizens irrespective of class or intelligence; in other words, in the final count on personal and human grounds first and foremost, though they may also seek to show that selection examinations of all kinds are socially wasteful of talent and human potential.

The cause of the person as against the machine can also be seen in the growing demands that institutions of higher education should give more freedom to the student to plan his own course of study, changing without too much penalty from one subject to another which in his own view may suit him better. The arguments in favour of a flexible system of credits for course units—whatever the arguments against— include the assumption that what he studies shall fit the student's needs as he perceives them so that what he spends most time on shall mean most to him personally. The widespread interest in Britain's Open University is in part due to the new opportunities it gives to many handicapped by lack of a fair chance earlier in life. All these tendencies have an element in them of defending people from being forced too narrowly into a mould, though they by no means necessarily include

3

overt criticism of the actual academic content or the professional orientation of university courses.

In the last few years especially a movement seems to have been gaining strength which openly takes more account of the affective elements in the human make-up and of their relation to the cognitive. Increasing numbers of teachers and students of applied subjects today are keen to safeguard their techniques from the de-humanising which may result from blindness in applying them. Concern about pollution and urban congestion have acted as catalysts. The condition of western man is now rapidly and consciously becoming one of estrangement in a world that has changed too quickly to enable him to find stable values in it. How to discover what can be valued or believed in except through personal experiences and reflection upon them? In many countries the life-style of the young both outside and inside their places of education has altered. That a new informality, a dropping of barriers between the classes and a new romanticism is represented in fashions of dress is not to be gainsaid; a still more significant index is the new openness in showing affection, especially towards the other sex; in the new attitude to the body; in the range of human causes being supported; and the emphasis being so powerfully put on process, involvement, personal relationships. A more engaged style is emerging.

Students in many countries criticise the university education they have received as too academic, too examination-minded, and as lacking relevance. With the vast increase in the numbers of students going to universities such criticism is not likely to grow less. But criticism of the students themselves whether as parts or as products of their universities comes from the public. They cost too much anyway. What do you get for all the money spent on them? Undergraduates waste a lot of their time and even when they take up jobs after graduating they tend to be disagreeably choosy and uppish. Clearly many students even in the past have lacked motivation for continuing academic study; drop-out rates remain too high for moral comfort even at the British thirteen to fourteen per cent (in some countries they are as high as forty five to fifty per cent), and students who have survived till their later undergraduate years are often more critical than they were at the end of their first year. There is evidence of intellectual and imaginative resources not cultivated; of uncertain aims; and of dissipated energies. Though for a generation a greatly increased proportion of people in positions of influence have been educated full-time to the age of twenty one or twenty two, the standards of taste manifest in advertisements, newspapers, films, theatres, T.V. programmes, the design of many office blocks and houses are low—in Britain, in the United States, in Japan, in France. The general picture must stand at least as an indictment of the power of the university graduate to affect his society. But more profoundly it may point to the ease with which the university product simply fits in with 'what goes', though he personally may read *The Times, Figaro, Commentary*, or *Asahi Shimbun* and in some cases be able pretty successfully to inoculate himself against the blandishments of the advertiser.

It is clear that many universities, apart from giving their major attention to research and the amassing of knowledge (which may very well be quite justified), have concentrated their best teaching efforts upon those they regard as their best students; either upon those already studying for higher degrees or those who give promise of developing a scholarly interest in a particular field. There are various ways in which a university department can become cosily insulated from the human world, and even from other departments in the university in which many of the undergraduates it is teaching may be spending a fair fraction of their time. Quite a proportion of professors are chiefly interested in clever students, and where the university is taking not two per cent but ten or fifteen per cent of the age group, only a minority can possibly be clever in the professor's understanding of the term.

Some of the questions about universities which most worry men are at bottom not really questions about the university but about life today. The university is an institution which can be attacked—and often unfairly—because it exemplifies or brings into the open some deep-seated conflicts of objective or belief which can be more successfully concealed in the pre-occupations of everyday. Its own multiplicity and diversity of aim embodies the incoherence of modern man. We lack the unity ourselves which men had in simpler times.

Surely the university should be less fallible, it is argued. After all, its members comprise a considerable proportion of the most self-aware and most intelligent people in the community. Not merely are they likely to be in some—even if limited—ways perspicacious, but they are by the very nature of their occupations sufficiently removed from the toil and stress of the market place, the factory, the chores of house-keeping, to be free to think more than most other people about major questions. They ought to be solving them for us. University teachers are reasonably well paid, have longer vacations than are yet common, and are not under so many concealed threats from their employers as most men are. This may make them envied; their detachment from the 'system' also makes them a little, even if only a little, more immune to the wiles of the salesman and the politician. Universities are obviously in a position of privilege. Yet they do so little to supply any of our needs except those for material progress.

Somewhere within every man is an inkling that to be merely a consumer of material goods is not enough: he is half-aware of the superficiality of the goal. Prosperity, a future filled to the brim with gadgets and goodies, cannot be entirely satisfying to anyone with a mind. But if the prosperous professor says nothing, fits in with the chase for national, even international, economic success, or conspicuously appears to do so, is he not just conspiring with everybody else to kill our conscience?

There is another way in which universities, because of the plurality of purpose and objective within society itself, can raise our conflicts into the light of day and find themselves shot at from both sides. If they accept contracts for research into, say, defence, or banking methods, or improved chemical fertilisers, we can charge them with compromising with a *status quo* that is corrupt and in which we ourselves may at times feel a little uncomfortable, even if not positively guilty. Such institutions, it is felt, ought to know better than to compromise with the powers that be. If, on the other hand, they refuse to accept such research contracts, they can be accused of wanting to sabotage the nation, of disloyalty, of not caring whether they increase unemployment, or of being willing to make food supplies less abundant than they might have been.

It is not of course only senior members of universities who disturb public equanimity, both apparent and real, but even more it is junior members. Universities contain many of the most articulate people in the age group eighteen to twenty two and give them a chance of being outspoken, non-conformist, as well as plain silly, in a way much resented by many outside the universities—including indeed many of the contemporaries of the students who are there. It can be pointed out with justice that some students in the universities are not working hard enough or they would not have so much free time in which to protest, rebel, condemn so many other people rather than themselves, even appear, whether as hippies or apathetics, to trade out of the whole situation: political, national, even human.

Most of us would indignantly deny that our own inner conflicts are in any way stirred up by student behaviour. And of course many people do not let conflicts within themselves influence their judgement of students. But the protests against the rat-race of modern life which some students conspicuously indulge in, however misguided their methods, are protests against an evil that is real and in fact recognised as such by many people of all ages. We may rightly have noted the exhibitionism, rowdiness, and inept planning of student marches and countermarches; but that human life itself should be a faster and faster rat-race, should spell more and more consumption *ad infinitum*: this we all really find unacceptable, however successfully we brush the problem under the carpet and diligently amass the money with which to buy bigger and thicker carpets under which to brush it.

The university thus in conspicuously symbolising some of the deficiencies of our society can serve as a target as convenient as politicians, or civil servants, or the clergy, or capitalists. It is more identifiable than many of the institutions within which such people hide themselves away; and some men are the more disappointed in it because the hopes and expectations they had invested in it were—legitimately it seemed—deeper than those they had invested, materially or otherwise, in big business or even in governments. They looked to it for the rescue of society and of the individual from the chaos which threatens us all, for a rescue to be accomplished through fundamental brainwork—on the one hand by science and applied science, through research and its application, by those who could work out better methods of agriculture, business administration, road construction, and so on; on the other hand by clarifying social objectives with the thoughtful help of philosophers, sociologists, historians, anthropologists and psychologists. Thirty years ago it was hoped that universities could educate a new generation of young people to take stock and to take a grip of themselves too. And they have demonstrably proved unequal to the task! What now?

When you ask the universities: What kind of human being do you really want to produce? the reply tends to come in instrumental terms. 'We are producing economists, technologists, surgeons, computer scientists and a thousand other specialists who can use their minds skilfully.' The overt demand from industry and governments is certainly for more and more men and women whose intellectual abilities can be used instrumentally. Today many 'hands' are 'brains', though they may often still be treated as hands used to be. In some ways this works quite well, whatever the compromises involved: for universities are rather good at educating experts capable of handling with intelligent detachment both things and ideas, and by no means so good at educating people.

But is such detachment, seen as an end in itself and not as a necessary stage on the way to something more inclusive, any longer viable? 'I am in favour of intellectual education', said a bright young university professor to me recently, 'because I am not confident enough of my moral and personal position to be in favour of anything else.' It will hardly be denied that the collapse in consensus about what human beings ought to be trying to become, indeed what their potentialities are, is very widespread in the world. The collapse of this consensus, our uncertainty about what human life can mean, leads on to, and is another name for, the collapse of authority—the external authority which people reject out of hand and the more inward authority, of 'conscience', which they fail to recognise. It is easier of course in such circumstances to concentrate on producing and employing experts, on making and investing money, on inventing new mechanisms, and on space exploration; and both our universities and our society, understandably, are loyally engaged in forwarding concerns of these sorts. But is this enough?

It is about all this that some of the better students are worried, and fundamentally because of this syndrome some of them want to participate in university government so as to change the whole set-up. The period of intense campaigning of 1968-70 may be over, but the desire is unchanged and so is the conviction of its rightness. Of course there are a thousand motives for wanting to participate, many of them crude products of self-interest. A simple seeking for power is one of them; a desire to dominate and get one's own way regardless; a wish to escape from hard intellectual work; sheer delight in violent talk and violent action for their own sakes; a distrust of those who appear to rule the roost with such little understanding; and so on. Motives are mixed and participation can mean such very different things to different people that the term itself becomes vague—and suspect.

'What can we trust? Whom can we trust?' These are basic questions for the young in a fluid and permissive society, which changes its standards with the flow of time and as the whirlpools of fashion revolve. 'We can trust our own experiences', seems to many the best answer. 'We want to make the university a more human place.' 'We want to participate in its whole life, so as to enable it to meet human needs, so that it will produce more than experts, will produce, maybe, more people who, whether they work or not, will love and care.' Some of the overtones indeed are Freudian rather than Marxian: Freud's twin tests of the good life were that a man should be able to love and to work.

So that it may not so much be participation in the committee work of the university that students want as, much more deeply, so considerable an involvement in its power structure that they can transform it—and with that, they hope, begin the transformation of our whole society. It is an idealist, and even in some sense a religious, movement that they have joined. Their reason for beginning with the university is the classic motto 'Start where you are'. Is this, though, a good place from which to begin? They have not calculated the odds; but some of them are a hundred per cent sure that universities need saving from becoming too much like conveyor belts, instead of communities of people who share values and causes together.

The answer on the part of universities to such student attitudes and idealism up to now is to put some students on to committees so that what they say can at least be heard. During recent years there have been quiet, but remarkable, moves in many universities to add students not merely to minor committees—such as library committees, timetable committees, committees on student discipline—but major ones also. In several universities now a few students sit on the Senate, in a small number of universities and colleges two or three students already sit on the Governing Body itself. And so far, by and large, universities appear pleased with the result.

But the criticism from the students' side is that as yet in few places has a meaningful number of students been given a chance of participating. If universities are to be changed in outlook in the radical way that is needed, they say; if students are to be really involved in their transformation, they may need to occupy half at least of the seats of power. 'By student decision-making I mean votes', says the radical. In other words, the university is under threat; but what is it proposed to put in its place? Often the radicals have no idea. First get rid of these evil places is the attitude of a few of the more extreme: only then can we build anew.

What is the response from public opinion to such views? 'Let the young go out into the world and work', some say. 'It would do them good and be better for the country.' Maybe for a number of students this could be the recipe. But such a reply does not face the facts, and the facts as they increasingly will be. No sensible person, however dissatisfied with the universities, really wants to scrap them altogether. He may want, if he is a prime minister, or a state governor, or a businessman, to reduce their number or size, their student intake, the amount of money they spend, their stand-offishness; to reform their method of government. But it is reform and not abolition which he seeks. And if the universities are curtailed in the process of reform, he certainly wants other institutions of tertiary education to fill the gaps.

Before we go on to consider in more detail what the problems are and what reforms might be called for, there are three things that must be said about the need for expanding tertiary education in general. First, every country which has offered a period of secondary schooling following a period of elementary, has found not merely that more and more children find it natural to go on to secondary school but that a higher and higher proportion stay there longer. The demand for a *chance* to go to university is likely to become greater the more pupils stay at their high school or their secondary school to the age of eighteen or so and do reasonably well there. Secondly, in an increasingly technological age there will be fewer and fewer jobs for the unskilled as the years go on. The amount of intellectual training required for an increasing proportion of the posts which have interest or bring power will call for a tertiary education not necessarily in the university but not exclusively of a narrow technical kind. Thirdly, and in the long run much the most important, more and more leisure is likely to be available in future for a large proportion of the population, skilled and unskilled. The difficulty is how to share it out more equitably so that much of it does not take the form of unemployment. The average paid worker, however, already has a good deal more leisure—including longer holidays— than he had twenty five years ago, and the average housewife too.

One of the difficulties is securing that far more people discover how to spend their leisure increasingly well and to like doing it. To indulge excessively in drugs can be a way of putting oneself more or less pleasantly to sleep, almost literally of killing time. Making use of others or oneself by frequent sex, by over-eating and drinking or 'going places fast', may all be thrilling and pleasurable, but what else are they? The challenge is how to find ways of using free time to enhance potential and raise quality of life. Any kind of tertiary education, including that given within universities, ought without doubt to be doing something for the majority of its students which helps to meet such a challenge. Most people fifty years from now are hardly likely to have to work—or to be working —for more than 850 hours in any year at the job which produces their main income for them.

The second solution to the problem of the university proposed in a number of European countries is that many more young men and women—fifteen per cent or twenty per cent of the age group—instead of going to universities, which might take ten per cent or less, should go to institutions of higher education of a less 'noble' or intellectually demanding sort. Successful completion of courses at these would, it is contended, lead on to jobs that require in reasonable moderation a trained intelligence and would be reasonably interesting, even if not, in so high a proportion of cases, of the prestige-bringing kind which the products of the universities may aspire to. There are powerful arguments in favour of such a policy, but even if the number of jobs to be filled by such usefully educated people remains high, will not these 'second tier' institutions of higher education inevitably find themselves faced with many of the same underlying problems as the universities, with a curriculum becoming more inclusive and more sociologically oriented? After all, as time goes on they will find themselves surrounded by much the same social environment as the universities—an environment demanding much more mobility, and offering greatly increased leisure, with most people able to read and converse in more than one language—and taking many of the same sorts of young people. Admittedly, they may tackle the task more effectively; but the problems themselves are not likely to go away. They may escape from some of the dangers which too much freedom is said to have brought to the universities, but if they are to be more circumscribed in their range of concern would it be at the behest of big business, the service industries, or the state? They are going to be more useful in what they can produce than the universities have been. Very likely. But what is meant by 'useful'? And who is to determine the limits of 'usefulness'? And, incidentally, will not some of the best of their teachers be likely to become discontented and less efficient if they are not allowed, if they wish, to spend time in researching and publishing, as university teachers do?

The question has also to be asked, quite seriously, whether any state can really afford to duplicate the immensely expensive and sophisticated equipment which the more advanced study and teaching of technology increasingly requires, including the computers, the special collections of books or records, the general library services and so on. Will not these things all increasingly have to be shared and, if so, is it not probable that relations between universities and other places of higher education will need to become closer? There is little logic in divorcing universities too completely from other institutions whose educational problems are the more similar the deeper one digs.

It has to be borne in mind too that it is becoming more and more difficult to separate out the technological from the technical, and jobs which require 'first tier' expertise from those which require only 'second tier'. There has been a phenomenal increase since 1950 or so in many advanced countries of commitment to applied science. Whole new

13

industries have been created and continue to be created. Electro-optics, xerography, the study of lasers, oceanography, are all developing rapidly, and thousands of new products are emanating from established industries—electronics, synthetic fibres, plastics, transport, photography. But the line between research and development, between inventiveness and application, becomes more difficult to draw with any firmness in most of them—as it does also between good 'elementary' and good 'secondary' teaching, between planning and the implementation of planning which captures the essence and spirit of what was intended, and between national and local administration that are creatively interrelated.

I am not arguing for a fusion of universities with other places of higher education, but for an increasingly close relationship between them. If places of tertiary education other than universities are to be created on a large scale, as is inevitable, they too will need to take seriously the responsibility for educating people with a sense of purpose, open to experience and able to judge the worth of their experience, as well as possesssed of expertise.

In so technological a civilisation as the one we live in, we cannot do without many trained people to serve our needs, or without many educated, responsible people to inspirit, to manage and administer the country, to see a sense of purpose in human life. How can we attain them? How can we deepen the tertiary education we give so as to be saved from the meaninglessness and de-humanisation that threatens? Can any institutions of higher education really fill that sort of bill? Could the universities conceivably change their outlook and presuppositions enough to do it? After all, they have evolved through many stages over the centuries. Can they evolve rapidly enough in the next thirty years to give the kind of lead which they are—by implication at least—being asked to give? Or, if not, can polytechnics or some other institutions for higher education take over—not contenting themselves with a utilitarian and technical role, but developing into places more centrally in touch with the national life, able to make a more profound and broadly based contribution of thought and insight than they have yet seen it as their function to do?

Universities are gradually realising that a change of scale involves also a change of character. The higher the proportion of the population involved in higher education the greater the extent to which universities, as well as the other places which give it, become emmeshed in the problems of the society of which they are now so obvious a part. No university can stand aside if it covers 500 acres and has 10 000 students, in the way it might have done when it was tiny.

In this chapter we have suggested that the university is under attack from a number of quarters. Some of the challenges may be short term; others are longer in range. The chief danger to universities at a time when civilisation itself is between two worlds may spring from their own contentment with giving an education that is too little concerned to develop either human understanding or moral responsibility. Yet if they fail here, they fail to meet some of the deepest needs both of society and of their own students, and may be the less able to resist, or be justified in resisting, the demand that they shall make themselves much more immediately useful in producing efficiently larger numbers of the well-equipped experts that society undoubtedly needs.

The threat of compelling them to evolve towards making themselves more useful in a fairly immediate way is compounded by the need to save money on higher education which is already obvious in Britain, the United States and many other countries, and likely to continue throughout the 1970s at least. The whole process must be made cheaper unless we are to deny rights and 'go back on democracy'. And the obvious way to make it cheaper is by cutting the length of courses, by reducing further the leisure which students have had (though so rarely used) for reflection, by making some of their university education part-time and more of it simply utilitarian.

It may help us to see the nature of this dilemma more clearly if we look at the route along which universities have come.

Chapter 2

Universities and their Environment: Mediaeval to Mid-20th Century

In the Middle Ages, when universities first developed in so many European countries, they were no doubt in a sense places of useful, professional training. But it was training given inside a culture that, unlike our own, was unified and pervasive —its purposes and sensibilities accepted unconsciously but by almost everyone. These presuppositions were largely taken for granted in universities, which in any case were small; but they played their part, as did the monasteries, in giving the culture an intellectual base. In mediaeval times, of course, only a fraction of young people received any kind of formal education, and it was only a tiny proportion of those who went on from school to university. In most cases it was from a school closely connected with the church that they went. The job of the mediaeval university in Europe was to produce a number of the professionals which contemporary society needed: to be lawyers, clergy, doctors, civil servants, scholars. Most of the ablest students who graduated from it went out into the world: the material rewards for staying on to teach in the university itself were certainly lower. The universities played no part in the world of work—which was largely agricultural or domestic and manual—and had little to do with the teaching of technical 'experts'. Their function was to study and teach: it was an intellectual function and they were international in their remit. Thomas Aquinas studied at the Universities both of Naples and Paris; Roger Bacon was both at Oxford and Paris.

And theirs were among the seminal minds of the Middle Ages.

Most students at mediaeval universities normally lived away from home. Some universities attracted outstanding students in certain fields, especially professional fields, because they had outstanding teachers in the central subjects. The mediaeval grapevine was an extraordinarily healthy plant; the absence of newspapers, radio or glossy prospectuses did not prevent students hearing of the distinction of Irnerius as a teacher of Law at Bologna, or the vivacity of the teaching of philosophy at Paris or Valladolid. But all the universities were essentially parts of a stable society, in which rate of change was slow. Sharp and violent though quarrels were between town and gown, there was little inclination on the part either of townsmen or gownsmen to question the fundamental right of the church to supply an underlying ideology about the nature of God and man. The mediaeval mind was not as introspectively critical or as individualised as the modern. It rejoiced in intellectual complexities and ramifications; but to the modern mind mediaeval poetry, art, even theology, seem curiously externalised, leaving the self unattacked and uninvolved. How many angels *can* dance on the point of a pin? Does it now seem in the least important to decide how many? Assumptions fostered by the church and by religion were taken for granted, as was travel freely across national boundaries within Christendom. The church stood behind the university as she did behind society. However bitter the disputes between Abelard and his opponents—whether philosophers or theologians— they all accepted God as First Cause and the source of truth. It was important to understand truth; but the way to it was not by questioning everything; rather by further exploration into the text of the Bible, the Fathers, into Aristotle, by logical deductions according to the rules, and by careful comparison of what the commentators had said. That life had a meaning, that it was not a mere progress or a mere deception, went undoubted. And it is their environment as a whole—mental as well as physical—that will determine what men will find it relevant, important, and in the long run *possible*, to study.

Universities themselves were not in mediaeval times very efficient places, either in teaching or learning. Those run by their students, after the Bologna model, may often have been more effective at teaching in ways that interested the learners than those run by masters, after the Paris model. But there can be little doubt that the influence of tutor or teacher on undergraduate and graduate alike was sometimes great. The teachers who were most influential were primarily so because they were authorities on what was the truth; only secondarily because they were technical experts in one or other branch of scholarship. They were also sometimes, no doubt, friendly human beings. Colleges served not only as very necessary protectors of their often youthful inhabitants, but as communities which had an interior influence upon many of them. The forms which examinations took are significant of the age itself: they were oral and the degrees awarded were with few exceptions unclassified. At each stage in the examining procedure examiners and candidate came face to face. But getting a degree was by no means for all the chief object of having a period at a university. The personal, theological and social elements in the education the mediaeval university gave were closely interwoven.

The Middle Ages were perhaps enchanted—so, it may be, are all ages, though the nature of the enchantment differs. In a mediaeval university town, with its bells and its churches, its frequent Saints' Days (on which lectures were totally suspended), its frequent funerals (the average length of people's lives was much shorter than now), with its teaching of astrology, it was not difficult to have a sense of unseen forces at work. The learning that went on was certainly not only cognitive.

One mark of the coming of the Renaissance is the decline in this corporate, unconscious, cultural consensus and an increase of individualism. Among the earliest evidences of this increase are the searchings for self-knowledge through the confession, through autobiography and through friendship about which Colin Morris (1972) has written so illuminatingly. But in general the emphasis on the importance of the individual's beliefs was a post-Reformation one. The Protestant religion came to attach much importance to individual belief— more than to the corporate acceptance, even recital, of the Creed. At the same time emphasis was put upon the experimental method for the discovery by the individual of objective facts about the world. This individual quest for truth showed itself in one direction by the effort to discover more about the contents of the earthly world and the way in which things behaved and to perfect the means for doing so. The method of science is one of directed observation and the invention of instrumentation interacted with cogwheeling effect upon the explorations men could make. It was the invention of the refracting telescope, and of a compass which allowed for magnetic declination, which enabled them to voyage so much further so much more safely. The method of science was one of proof by demonstration. It used the touchstone of observed fact but also the touchstone of reason; truths had to match the facts but also to be consistent with one another. The search of post-Reformation man for truth was, however, shown in another direction too: by internal exploration and an individual searching of the Bible for truth ('the priesthood of all believers'); a searching within for principles ('conscience') and illumination ('the inner light'). In other words its sphere was a seeking of the evidence from personal experience; the test was a group consensus at a certain level that the experiences which members had were genuine, profound, mutually supportive and therefore consonant with reason too. This groping towards the idea that there were two *kinds* of test of what was consistent with truth and reason is of high import. Its significance has perhaps not even yet been fully appreciated.

It is fascinating to trace, with help from the Oxford English Dictionary, the divergence in meaning between the words *experiment* and *experience* from the fourteenth to the eighteenth century. In the late fourteenth century the words experience and experiment were still used, to all intents and purposes, in exactly the same sense. They denoted the action of putting to the test, a tentative procedure, proof by actual trial. Whereas in 1382 Wyclif wrote 'Now y schal take experyment of you' we find him in the 1388 edition of the same work just substituting the word experience for the word experiment. Spenser's *Faerie Queene* in 1596 says 'She caused him to make experience upon wild beasts'. It is not until the seventeenth century that the words begin to be used with an approach to their modern differentiation of meaning. Thus by 1674 the word experience has come to include, for the first time, the meaning 'a state of mind or feeling forming part of the inner religious life', as a quotation dated 1674 from Owen's *Holy Spirit* suggests: 'Testified unto by the experience of them that truly believe'—a sense of the word that Bunyan also employs. But by the same date the word experiment has acquired the meaning of 'the process or practice of experimentation' and in 1678 Russell's *Gebir* says 'This is proof by experiment' and in the mid-eighteenth century Watts in his *Improvement of the Mind* says 'This sort of observation is called experiment'. Since the mid-eighteenth century the words have virtually had their modern meaning. Experiment has become identified with operations conducted in a scientific frame of mind; experience has a much more personal and internal meaning. Experiences may be introspected. Experiments may not.

But scientific study was not advanced within the universities as such—conservative institutions that they were—although among those most keenly involved in experimentation were some university graduates and undergraduates, including graduates in the oldest university subjects, especially medicine. It was the quest for objective truth about the physical world which was the animating principle behind the scientific inquiries which began to spread all over Europe. And the proof was by repeated test: if an experiment conducted in exactly the same way a thousand times yielded exactly the same result, man had good cause for confidence in it. If laws could be logically deduced to explicate such demonstrable behaviour on the part of bodies or objects there was a *prima facie* justification for thinking those laws sound.

The universities, however, had little to do with the manifold discoveries made by science and its methods between 1600 and 1800—even though the imaginative researches involved were often done by university graduates. The universities continued to train the 'establishment' but neither their curricula nor their teaching methods were adapted so that they came to be in the forefront either of intellectual inquiry or of its technological application.

Most European universities, whether they were chiefly collegiate as at Louvain or St Andrews or chiefly non-collegiate as in Copenhagen or St Petersburg or Leiden, continued in fact to function along mediaeval lines until the nineteenth century. Church influence continued to be strong; there was an element of retreat from the world even in those which were not collegiate or residential. The basic dependence as far as curriculum was concerned was on classics, pure mathematics, philosophy, theology—and they continued to produce clerics, lawyers, some men of philosophic mind, the occasional scholar; though medical doctors too. Even in 1800 the countries of Europe were of course still overwhelmingly agricultural communities. The growth and transformation of the cities which proceeded in the first half of the nineteenth century, with the rapid building of factories, the application to them of steam power, the growth of transport facilities, for the most part left the universities on one side. But so had the introduction of new methods regarding the growing of crops. The universities had neither the Departments of Pure Science nor of Technology to help; nor were many of them as yet serious centres of scientific research. With the transformation of western society, however, by the spread of industrialisation, came the demand for the application of science and its discoveries to technical accomplishment. How could the universities, as such, again play a leading part in society?

Humboldt's University of Berlin, founded in 1809, set an example that was followed: but it did not come into existence in order to be at the service of industry. Its professors were devoted to pure research, not to finding out more truth that would have a profitable pay-off. There was as aristocratic an element in the Humboldt type of pure research university, centred on the laboratory, as there was in the continuing concept of a university devoted to scholarship, as at Paris, or a university, as at Oxford and Cambridge, given over to the teaching of young men in subjects far removed from any industrial application at all.

The rise of the University of Berlin and the effects of its example on the development of research in other German universities attracted students from far and wide. A research method pursued with this new intensity was a break-through, intellectually inviting and of promise at a period when industry, population—and colonial empires—were all building up.

Among the students attracted to Germany were sizeable numbers from an America filled with an energetic spirit of practical enterprise and anxious to break from English leading strings. They took back with them to the U.S. new insights into the potentiality and serviceability of the research method. Both Germany and the United States began to find an almost priceless asset in the harnessing of scientific investigation to industrial use. The possibilities began to be widely seen—and seized—both in Europe and the United States of using the discoveries of science for the direct service of a technological society. The concept was born and developed of the university as a service institution: intelligent, useful, eager to go more or less in the direction society wanted, and indeed to lead it further in that direction. The creation in the U.S. of Land Grant universities was a highly significant step in this process. With the passing in 1862 in the U.S. of the Morrill Act, grants of land of up to 30 000 acres were made available to a number of state colleges, giving them capital, but also incentive, to develop 'agriculture and the mechanic arts in their region'. The idea that universities could be of practical benefit to the whole community received a fillip the more powerful as the value of the land itself grew over the years. As the century went on, the growth of highly intelligent scientific research in many European universities was linked with industrial applications in more and more cases. Technische Hochschulen developed in Germany. Applied mathematics in particular was seen to be of great importance. Some of the newly founded university institutions in England in the latter part of the nineteenth century or the earliest part of the twentieth developed Departments such as those for Textiles and Colour Chemistry at Leeds, Shipbuilding at Newcastle upon Tyne, Glass Technology at Sheffield, Metallurgy and the Biochemistry of Brewing at Birmingham; and technical institutions outside the universities proper proliferated.

Since 1850 universities in many countries have come more and more to minister to the needs of an industrial age—by applying science, economics, mathematics and later psychology and sociology to its requirements, with research as the main instrument. The humanities to a considerable extent have been carried along in this rushing slipstream and have themselves aimed at the production of busy research workers. The external environment has become urban; the social climate secular. This still developing state of things has been helped by a number of factors: the momentum and energy which increasing power to control the world has brought; an insufficient awareness on the part of intellectuals, as well as men generally, of the sheer importance of sensibilities and underlying attitudes; the subservience of women and the feminine; the non-recognition of the difference made to what might be called the ecological balance of the life of the mind by a city existence, increasingly competitive, decreasingly intimate, friendly or kind; the growth of competitive and economic nationalisms; and the tendency to throw out religion altogether when its credal formulation had become inadequate.

What of the appeal to the authority of experience rather than of experiment? The acceptance of the reasonableness of such an appeal was never quite lost in the English university circles even in the eighteenth century, as Wesley's famous sermon on suffering, preached at the University Church, St

Mary's, at Oxford in 1739 bears witness, or the poetry of Gray, later Professor of History and Modern Languages at Cambridge, written in the mid-century. And early in the next century it was at the universities that Coleridge and Shelley—drop-outs though they were—mixed with groups of more or less like-minded undergraduates, introspective, philosophical, idealist, impractical. Wordsworth was a Cambridge man; so in the first third of the nineteenth century was Tennyson with a group of 'The Apostles' around him. The college must have been a centre for experience where moments of insight came to many undergraduates in Newman's words, 'one by one', but the legitimacy of those insights came to be recognised by others as well as themselves. The defence of the college as an educative medium was indeed that you lived in a community that meant a lot to you personally: it was not merely the teaching that you received but the spirit of the place that would matter to you. Victorian Balliol, intellectual and selective in membership, was the epitome of the college ideal, and it is notable that when in this century in Britain the attempt came to revive the college concept, at Keele in North Staffordshire, it was the Balliol influence that was predominant. And it was undergraduate education that was at the centre. In the twentieth century, indeed, the—perhaps temporary—revival of the idea of the college is not unconnected with a protest against an over-emphasis on research-mindedness.

But the major effort of the twentieth century has undoubtedly been to develop more universities of a technological kind and to emphasise within existing universities the parts which were likely to be of use to society in a fairly immediate sense. This is the dominant tradition and we owe it a great deal. The control of chance has been seen as the chief means of improving the human lot—with the controllers welcomed and indeed found indispensable to human progress, whether engineers, sociologists or 'value-free' investigators of a hundred kinds.

During our own century places of higher education, and particularly universities, have at least until recently grown in power by leaps and bounds. A greater and greater proportion of the most intelligent young in every advanced country have been going on to tertiary education, whether or not efficiently selected and whether or not adequately financed to do so. Any deficiencies in scope in the outlook of universities (or of the higher technical institutions) are therefore in danger of being transferred to a greater and greater proportion of the population. Even the most thoughtful and perceptive of such students, who ought to have been able to articulate different assumptions and a different outlook, run the risk of being unconsciously converted to the current orthodoxies and trends. The numbers who now exhibit so excessive and so unexamined a faith in economics and the social sciences—indispensable though both are to man's future—are a case in point. Moreover universities in most countries already control school syllabuses at the secondary stage without in the least adequately realising the de-sensitising and subtle effects of their doing so.

The general assumption has grown that the only kinds of knowledge which are the proper concerns of higher education are 'hard' knowledge—factual, cognitive, directly or indirectly useful. Now of course it can be contended that higher education will best serve the purposes of mankind, at any rate at present, if it is thus limited in scope. But if this is so, what institutions can we develop which will have more comprehensive purposes in mind? If any new institution, wide and deep in its mental and human concerns, comes into being it will find that intelligent young men and women of eighteen to twenty two are among the archetypal and most capacious representatives of humanity with whom it must be in touch.

A university, I suggest, cannot serve even its own society adequately if its understanding of the scope of knowledge is confined to those kinds which are external and explanatory or if its picture of human nature and human problems is limited to the contemporary. It should, through its departments and their interrelationships, give attention to learning and teaching about things that matter without undue regard to a merely present-day estimate of the things that matter most. But if that is too idealist and impracticable, at least a university must be aware of human needs and interests over as wide a range as possible. Scientific research, mathematical, historical, and other sorts of scholarship, would be very much its province, but it will also take into account more interior ways of knowing which are part of the human heritage: aesthetic, moral, religious. It is, as Coleridge said, 'a mistake to try to shape convictions and deduce knowledge from without by an exclusive observation of outward and sensible things as the only realities'.[1]

The stress we place upon the accurate, the detailed and the measurable, important though they are to any civilised existence, is one of the factors which can lead to an under-estimate of the continuing needs of students for a broadly varied general education and to a lack of perception of the significance of the creative arts. The more complex the devices and organisation of a technological world, the more indispensable research and therefore research-mindedness become— with highly trained people alone able to take a number of the decisions which so greatly affect everybody, or invent and use the hardware with which to implement them. But while universities with their analytic temper have been growing rapidly in power in our own century, institutions and customs which served as canals and reservoirs of the inward, feeling, life, and of sensibility, have tended to decline. The churches have become weakened and theology is becoming typically a study of other people's faiths, not one's own. Once, for many people, hymns gave

> '. . . darkness some control
> and left a loophole for the soul'.[2]

The traditions of spontaneous folk-song, of good design in houses and implements, of the natural greetings and good manners which indicated an ordered social life and which

1 *The Friend*, II, 10.
2 Robert Lowell.

stemmed back to feudal times and an era of the village, have naturally and inevitably become exhausted. The family, though still retaining great power, was becoming by the 1940s weakened by the impact, which parents found it hard to control and impossible to negate, of radio and T.V. programmes coming right into the living room, the impersonality and noise of town and factory life, blocks of flats to live in, and quick facilities for travel to take one away from the home. The slow influence which the great events of suffering, birth, old age and death, if they are reflected upon, can exert so powerfully, can be impaired by clinical attitudes and the easy shutting of the heart they can breed. The hospitalisation of the old and the sick can in the interests of hygiene and comfort also remove potent reminders of human fragility. Very much in all this change of custom and circumstance was of course to be welcomed. The interest, vitality and excitement of daily living has been enhanced for millions during our century. But the impoverishment and atrophy of sensibility is a human deprivation.

It becomes imperative, however, this being the state of affairs, that universities and other places of higher education should take much more heed of the ecology of the mind as a whole and of human motivation, seeing to it that the life of the feelings is not starved or neglected, but educated and disciplined. Later in the book we shall be considering some of the implications and the practicalities of this. Scientists at least as much as many of those who study the humanities and the arts are increasingly aware of the problem.

It is not to be overlooked that even in the nineteenth century, when universities were being more and more influenced by the industrial and developmental needs of their countries, many elements were still preserved of a 'pure', intellectual, non-technical character—if too few which sought to discipline heart and mind *together*. Underneath, though at times rather far underneath, a current continued to flow which involved an appeal to private and personal experience and a test of its authority by consensus and tradition. Throughout the nineteenth century in, for instance, the English and German and Spanish universities, there were individuals and groups who incarnated this movement. It was represented by Wordsworth and Coleridge and Matthew Arnold, Goethe and Schleiermacher, Hegel and Unamuno, Kierkegaard and Ortega.

Chapter 3

The Problem Sharpens: The 1940s to the 1960s

I

The grip on British universities of life in a technological world was made more immediate and inescapable by the urgent needs of the country as it fought the war of 1939-45—for a period almost in isolated combat with the enemy. The country began to find its universities useful in a hundred ways not clearly recognised or appreciated before. I can illustrate this from personal experience.

It was early in 1940, when the Second World War was beginning to hot up, that I was asked to take the place of the Registrar of the University of Durham.[1] Both the real Registrar and his Deputy had departed on government service and the theory was that as the war went on fewer and fewer students would be enrolled and the administrative burdens be about right for an amateur to carry; and so I was seconded from the academic staff to take their places. But as the war continued the nation found its universities more and more indispensable to produce the technically qualified people it needed, to give advanced courses to men in the forces and to conduct researches vital to the war effort. When the war ended the University of Durham was catering for more students than at any previous time in its history.

During the war period many academics too, including some of the most able, were recruited as temporary civil servants

[1] The nearest American equivalent in terminology is perhaps Executive Vice-Chancellor.

and took up duty in London; and vice-chancellors of universities began to find themselves confidently consulted by numbers of government departments on questions of the production and training of specialists. The whole range of government departments which had before hardly found it necessary to be in touch with them now found it expedient to be so—from the War Office itself to the Ministries of Agriculture, Information, Health, Food and Labour. In brief the nation had finally become conscious that its universities were reservoirs of knowledge, ability and experience and were immense assets to it. They were service institutions on a large scale. Under these circumstances the Committee of Vice-Chancellors and Principals became a more essential and far more respected body than it had been before—a meeting place where the heads of universities could exchange views and work towards coherent policies, even though at no time did its members formally represent their institutions.

After the war there was a huge influx of students to the universities, many of them mature and responsible men and women with a background of national service, willing to work hard and with pent-up hope released. It was clear enough that to secure the supply of qualified people needed for various skilled jobs, far more planning was called for than in the amateurish pre-war world. Hence the setting up of various committees, composed largely of university people, to think out the requirements. There was the Barlow Committee on Scientific Manpower, for instance, which reported in 1946 that we should need by 1955 almost to double the number of graduate scientists we had hitherto thought it requisite to produce; the Goodenough Committee which replanned medical education and recommended a vast increase in the number of trained medicals; the Teviot Committee which declared that we should treble the annual entry to our dental schools. The suggestions of these committees were very largely acted upon, and acted upon speedily.

The University Grants Committee itself was in 1946 given

new terms of reference, broader than before, terms which were widened further in 1952. Its part in the planning process was made much clearer and its duties towards the nation on the one hand and the universities on the other more fully defined. Its new terms of reference (30 June 1952) were: 'To enquire into the financial needs of University education in Great Britain; to advise the Government as to the application of any grants made by Parliament towards meeting them; to collect, examine and make available information relating to University education throughout the United Kingdom; and to assist, in consultation with the Universities and other bodies concerned, the preparation and execution of such plans for the development of the Universities as may from time to time be required in order to ensure that they are fully adequate to national needs.' The amount of grant aid to universities from the nation was going up rapidly quinquennium by quinquennium, indeed year by year; and for the first time it added to its officers a full-time Deputy Chairman to attend more closely to the added problems of financial control which the apportioning of the larger grants involved. The change in the temper of the Grants Committee between the time when Sir Walter Moberly was its Chairman (1935-49) and that when the Deputy Chairman, Sir Arthur Trueman, succeeded him in the Chair, was marked. Under Moberly a good deal of the morning at each of the monthly meetings was occupied with what might be called policy questions—with their financial implications considered only subsequently, though seriously. Henceforward, and almost at once, questions of cost came further to the fore. The office staff was increased, though it was not until 1957 that the first of what is now a team of qualified architects was added to the U.G.C.'s own staff.

In the close relation between the universities and the nation, the assumption remained that the country's real needs were only those which the nation itself perceived. Of course, vice-chancellors, members of the Grants Committee, any professor or lecturer at any university, could express an opinion, and many did. But the money with which to do things increasingly

31

came from the State. There was astonishingly little interference, but also relatively little inquiry on anybody's part into the concept of 'national need' which bulked so large, or into the consequences for universities of the expanding range of their enterprises and of the subjects in which they were called upon to do serious research as well as teaching.

The slowly increasing availability of funds from national sources tended as a matter of fact to inhibit in some ways fundamental inquiries into the function of the university. During the post-war period numerous grants from Foundations were made to help research—usually specific researches involving experimentation. No English Foundation (Nuffield, Leverhulme, Wolfson were among the largest) had anything approaching the wealth of the great American Foundations (Ford, Carnegie, Rockefeller) or of the Gulbenkian. But American as well as British money was to be obtained by British university departments who could put up a good case, and who wished to investigate a problem or initiate a project according to a method with a fair promise of yielding hard evidence. Departments in medical schools, departments of chemistry, physics or geology, benefited greatly from such outside support, and incidentally added to their own prestige and power in the university. But practically no money was forthcoming, at any rate until after 1960 and not very much then, to encourage men to spend time in thinking about the purposes of the university itself, its teaching methods, its overall curriculum, its relations with the State or the outside world, or even to pursue inquiries into the concept of 'national need'. How could one 'research' into such fields anyway?

All the same, some anxieties were beginning to make themselves felt about the future of the university if its *raison d'être* was to serve a State whose wishes and will it might grow less and less able to influence. Some of these worries found expression in Moberly's own *The Crisis in the University* (1949) and others in publications such as Daniel Jenkins' *The Educated Society* (1966).

Some attempt to search for a practical answer to some of

such anxieties can be seen in the creation of the University College of North Staffordshire, opened in 1949, which later became the University of Keele, of which more will be said in Chapter 8. Many people who had little enthusiasm for this particular venture were nevertheless dissatisfied with universities as they were tending more and more to become— increasingly departmentalised, according less importance to the effectiveness of their teaching than to the quality of their experimental research, and above all not asking some of the major questions.

Throughout the 1950s there were advocates of policies, mistaken though some of them may have been, which aimed at keeping the universities humane in temper and less specialised in curriculum for more of their students. One line was in favour on many grounds of more residential provision for students, as witness the report on *Halls of Residence*, published by the U.G.C. (1957) itself, whose policy of grant aid for the building of halls raised the proportion of students in them from 27·3 per cent in 1956 to 35·1 per cent in 1966, in spite of the vast increase in total student population between those dates.[1]

A number of civic universities, beginning with Birmingham in 1947, made some attempt to persuade more students to read for less narrowly specialised degrees. They did this in two ways. One was by making it possible to take a B.Sc. or B.A. (General) with Honours, so that it was at least theoretically possible to have the same chance of getting first class honours if you combined three different subjects as if you specialised in one subject. The other way to get a good degree of wider range was by taking a Joint Honours course in a combination of two subjects—for example English literature and philosophy, Latin and history, psychology and music. But the pressures operating behind the scenes were discouraging: and relatively few students took advantage of such an opening. They found themselves not really belonging to an Honours School in so

1 Sources: *Halls of Residence*, Appendix I; *University Development 1962–1967*, Tables 7 and 8.

intimate a way as those who followed the more conventional path. It was, moreover, often excessively difficult to persuade the professors in charge that a First in a Joint Honours School should not demand almost as much work and ability as getting a First in both Schools separately would have done.

In the United States during the period 1945-60 universities found themselves increasingly under pressure to sacrifice independence to meet the demands of a technological society, dominated even more than the British by the interests—real and supposed—of the consumer. The definition of what were the national needs was voiced at this time, however, not so much by the State or public opinion as by big business. Funds were available favouring a concentration on the production of useful knowledge to be obtained by objective research, and these were channelled to university departments by the wealthy Foundations—only a trickle reaching the humanities as compared with the technologies, including medicine and surgery, or the pure sciences. Even the grants given to humanities favoured research which could be quantified or practically applied: 'Their greatest successes, in regard to humanities research', remarks Robert S. Morison (1964) in illustration, 'seemed to have been in the theory of linguistics and its application to language' (p. 1135). Grants of federal money increased but on condition that tasks should be undertaken which would benefit the country in specific ways, particularly in defence, health or welfare.

Reactions against the concept of the university as a place of experimentally validated knowledge alone are to be found in the continuing development during the 1950s of programmes involving more integrated and interdisciplinary studies at the undergraduate level—notably, the efforts made at Harvard following publication of the report *General Education in a Free Society* (1946). The influence of the work of Porter Butts of Wisconsin in the design and furnishing of university unions as cultural as well as social centres spread wide, while more and more universities found it possible to raise money with which to build residence halls of their own. In these the sexes were at this time segregated, usually by building, but sometimes by alternate floor (with separate elevators for the sexes, stopping at the appropriate floors!), but the idea of a combined residence hall with different wings in an X-formation, two wings each being occupied by the different sexes and with a large central coeducational common area, where the wings crossed, was exemplified at Indiana University and elsewhere.

II

The 1960s saw, particularly in the United States but also in Britain, a rocketing of student numbers. Total enrolment in all institutions of higher education in the United States rose from 3·8 million in 1960 to 8·5 million in 1970—the largest numerical increase ever experienced in one decade.[1] In Great Britain the number of full-time students in higher education rose from well under 200 000 in 1960 to some 400 000 in 1970.[2] There was an expansion of funding for higher education purposes during these years which even up to 1960 would have been regarded as quite beyond attainment. Cyclotrons, synchrotrons, large computers, are very expensive.

Early in the decade Sir Charles Morris (1962), then Vice-Chancellor of the University of Leeds, called pure science departments, and especially the physicists and chemists, 'the effective guardians of the conscience of the universities. They are themselves concerned with the pursuit of knowledge for its own sake; and they have the great advantage, perhaps a singular advantage, that they can reach the top of their own professional trees and gain the highest honours in the great world without derogating in any way from the purity of their concern with pure knowledge. They are today the true "naturals" of the academic world' (p. 26). In Britain it was they who insisted most strongly upon rigour in the testing of

---

1 Source: *New Students and New Places*, p. 11.
2 Sources: *Higher Education*, Appendix One, Table 46; *Higher Education Review*, Summer 1972, p. 34, Table 4.

evidence and on the necessity for properly specialist grounding in the particular science being studied. Subjects like the history of science or the philosophy of science, though slowly developing, were regarded by many science professors in Britain as frills or temptations to wander, rather than as of real importance for most students reading for Ph.D.s. 'The social responsibility of the scientist' was regarded rather as a headline appropriate for newspaper articles than as subject matter for a lecture course in, say, a chemistry or physics department. And departmentalism was still strengthening.

An innovation during the 1950s in Britain was the foundation of Colleges of Advanced Technology, intended to develop as centres for higher technological education. These, formed from ten of the largest technical colleges owned by local education authorities, were regionalised and given a higher status. The courses of lower standard for which they had previously been responsible, in addition to courses of approximately degree level, were removed from them and they were charged to develop their degree level work.

By the early 60s they were doing this so well that the Report (1963) of the Robbins Committee recommended (paras 392, 393) that they should become technological universities, a suggestion rapidly accepted by the government and implemented. But though this added necessary numbers to the technologists receiving higher education, in itself it did nothing to ensure an increase in the armies of well-educated technicians in which the nation was deficient. Moreover by 1965 more and more was being said about the sheer cost of higher education. Could not something be done to provide industry with large numbers of people well-equipped to serve it, really in touch with its needs, professionals rather than scientists perhaps, up-to-date accountants and executives rather than managers? Hence the proposal made in May 1965 by the Secretary of State for Education that a binary system of higher education should be created in Britain; the universities to comprise an autonomous sector and a set of institutions of further education to constitute a non-autonomous or public sector.

This proposal was followed a year later by the announcement that the government was establishing some thirty polytechnics, based upon specially chosen Colleges of Technology. The newly created polytechnics were founded on the strict understanding that none should become a university and that all should have part-time as well as full-time students, a number of lower level courses as well as higher ones. A wide variety of subjects is available for study up to degree level in the polytechnics, but all have a more or less practical bias. As yet comparatively little research is going on in them, though the pressure for permitting this is building up.

It is interesting to recall the arguments which were being adduced in the later 60s for and against expanding British non-university higher education on a really big scale. The arguments in favour were as follows:

1 We need to produce much larger numbers of highly trained, technically equipped people who have intelligence. Since there simply is not room for them in existing universities, the obvious places in which they should be educated are the regional and area technical colleges.

2 It would be far more expensive to train all these people in universities than in technical colleges, where the cost per student is lower, so we should develop our regional and area technical colleges as fast as we can, but as day colleges, providing residential halls only to the minimum extent and tutorial methods of teaching only in very limited degree. This would be a far wiser way of spending such money as can be afforded.

3 There is need for keeping higher education in much closer touch with industry, with the schools, with the needs of the people. We should, therefore, make much more resolute use of the vocational motive and develop the idea of sandwich courses, in which part of a student's course is taken in college, part or parts in a suitably chosen industry or job.

4 Universities have tended in the past to be somewhat snobbish, aristocratic in temper and academic in ways that clearly

are now dated. They are, in fact, hidebound. It might be better, even for the universities themselves, for a competitive system to be set up.

5 Britain's example to overseas territories in the inauguration of institutions of higher education has tended to be one of giving them expensive university institutions on a collegiate principle. The provision has too often been wasteful and irrelevant, made mainly because of the prestige of university institutions at home.

6 The Americans have much to teach us in these matters, and we ought to have more regard to it. They have not hesitated to develop degree-giving institutions in considerably greater variety than we have done, and it is the flexibility of their pattern that we need to bear in mind. In the United States, a student can graduate from a state college of agriculture or teaching, and go on, if he is good enough, to postgraduate work at a university. In Britain, he might have to start working for a first degree, even after gaining a thoroughly good diploma in agriculture, teaching, or social work, and only be allowed to study for a mastership if he obtained that degree with a high class of honours.

So much for the arguments on one side. But there were good arguments, too, for expanding higher education along more traditional lines:

1 Higher education, properly so-called, is far more than a technological training. The only institutions which, in fact, have so far given this with any success have been universities. It is universities which have the experience. They have at least sometimes in the past succeeded in giving an excellent technological training in a profoundly liberalising environment. It is undeniable that a high proportion of our best doctors, civil servants, research scientists, clerics, teachers, lawyers, are university products; and they have not merely an expertise but a broadmindedness and humanity which owe much to their university years.

2 If you are going to produce an educated man he must have been initiated into the whole complex of cultural traditions, learning subconsciously a whole hierarchy of value judgements as well as developing the ability to raise these into consciousness in order to examine, and, if necessary, correct them. He will best learn to do this in an environment which is itself nourished by a variety of disciplines; in which scholarship of many types flourishes, as does the self-awareness which scholarship brings. It is good, not bad, to have some impractical, self-aware, unworldly people about. The production of efficient business executives, computer technologists, advertising experts, even conscientious chemists, ought not to be the principal aim of an institution of higher education. These people are not the fine flowers of civilisation. An institution of higher education which produces no civilised, rather detached, untemptable élite is failing in one of its main purposes, however skilful it may be in producing useful functionaries for the laboratory, office, or classroom. For the sake of achieving this objective we must be prepared to sacrifice some lesser ones, even perhaps some material prosperity.

3 A higher education that is liberalising is most likely to be given in a physical environment that relieves the mind of the stresses, worries and ugliness of everyday living. Admittedly it is expensive to build colleges and campuses on the Oxford and Cambridge, Nottingham or Exeter pattern. But this is the ideal, and the nation should provide as many as it can afford. We must provide for our young guardians-to-be an environment that is as powerful in its good effect upon the subconscious mind as we can afford to make it. The kind of place for new institutions of higher education is in cathedral cities such as Canterbury, Norwich, and York rather than at places like Dagenham, Huddersfield, Stoke or West Ham, however efficient our regional technical colleges there may be.

To these arguments the advocates of a binary system of higher education reply: 'Do keep in touch'. Students themselves want their universities to be more democratic in times like ours; they don't *want* to be an élite: they are tired of being regarded as different from other people. Look at the way they dress. Cathedral cities are *passé*: this is the age of the high-rise building, not of the dreaming spire. We want more exports, more social surveys, more research which is going to be of some practical use. It is no good offering us your civilised, rather stand-offish, untemptable élite (people we don't much like anyway) if this means that we must sacrifice prosperity and comfort to produce them. We would undoubtedly prefer to have larger numbers of well-trained but efficient surgeons who are masters of their techniques than smaller numbers who are philosophers as well as being surgeons. It is no use offering our schools a smaller number of good quality teachers as a substitute for a much greater number of more ordinary, run-of-the-mill ones who can save people from being faced with classes of fifty or so to teach. In the last resort, we would rather have more of the average than fewer of the best. And there is no need to train most of the doctors, chemists, business executives or teachers we need in universities that are exclusive or detached or residential.

What is clear is that during the period 1960–70 the dominant emphases in higher education in Britain as a whole were increasingly in favour of developing the kind of graduate who would be useful and usable, 'knowing his stuff', and able to contribute, even if only down one or two circumscribed paths, to the nation's well-being; inquiring of mind; fined down by a research training if he were able enough to secure and profit from the still increasing number of scholarships and fellowships available for research. But it was not expected that his higher education would, except rather accidentally, make him far-sighted or contemplative. His job was to concentrate on sharpening his abilities to think and analyse. It was only on the side, if at all, that his experiential capacities might be developed, educated or disciplined.

But though these were the dominant emphases, the group of

new 'liberal arts and science' universities first mooted in the 1950s came actually into being in the 1960s and in a number of ways, at any rate to begin with, they stood for a somewhat different concept. The idea was that there should be some seven new universities, all starting at about the same time, built in attractive places, on rural parkland sites, but near cities of some character which could at the same time provide a number of student lodgings. These universities were expected to do some new things in higher education in Britain and not to be technological in their main emphasis. It was foreseen that they would to some extent be in competition with one another and that this might in itself be a stimulating state of affairs. The first of the seven, the University of Sussex, near Brighton, opened its doors in 1961 and between then and 1965 the others were begun—at York, in Essex near Colchester, in Kent near Canterbury, in East Anglia near Norwich, in Warwickshire near Coventry, and at Lancaster some three or four miles from the city itself. Later two other new universities with somewhat similar ideals were created: near Stirling in Scotland and near Coleraine in Northern Ireland.

Consciously or unconsciously the group was an attempt to revive a concept of the university as a place of spirited general education which, while not neglecting specialist study, would emphasise experiential as well as experimental capacities. Three—York, Kent and Lancaster—sought to be collegiate in physical pattern, but all sought to be collegiate in spirit. They tried to provide a more coherent curriculum, of which more will be said in Chapter 8, for their students, in most cases abandoning the old pattern of Faculties (arts, science, law, applied science, etc.) and substituting Schools of Studies, one of the objectives being to lessen the conservative force of the big departments and prevent too much power from getting into the hands of professors whose interests were subject-centred rather than institution- or even student-centred. They sought, as Asa Briggs, later Vice-Chancellor of the University of Sussex, said in an inspired phrase, 'to re-draw the map of learning' (1964) and by offering possibilities of combining different areas of study under a variety of coherent groupings to produce graduates who were more open to the world and keen to go on learning widely about it.

Nor were they unsuccessful in persuading a number of Foundations to support some of the new enterprise they were showing. Small at first, and owing some of their keenness no doubt to a sense that they were pioneers, they rapidly grew from institutions catering for a few hundred students to ones catering by 1971 for 3 600 at Sussex, 2 700 at East Anglia and 2 800 at Lancaster. And though they have relatively few research or Ph.D. students they have an appreciable number studying for masterships, including some for M.A. and M.Sc. degrees of a more broadbased kind than is conventional. They still tend to represent a minority movement among the universities of the country as a whole; none has a school of medicine, or of agriculture; only Warwick offers engineering on any scale. Departmental power in several is undoubtedly growing. They are not immune from the dangers of living in an industrialised, competitively-minded, consumption-obsessed age as the student unrest of 1968 and 1969 at Warwick and Essex, and that of 1971 and 1972 at Lancaster, showed. Nor have they found as yet the secret of producing any great proportion of students with 'a sense of values in an age of facts'. The bleak financial climate ahead may be especially hard in its effects upon them.

III

In the United States during the period 1960–70 one reason for the increase, not merely of undergraduate but also of graduate students, including particularly Ph.D.s, was the still growing conviction that a degree was now indispensable to any position of power or influence in the country and a passport, too, to most jobs which could yield even a moderate affluence. But there was a special reason for the burgeoning of the numbers studying for doctorates—which were certainly no easier to get than when the numbers seeking them were fewer. Whereas in

Britain it is possible—indeed almost a requirement—if a man or woman has intelligence to prove that fact by taking a first class honours degree at the end of an undergraduate course, in the U.S. the surest way of showing capability of an intellectual kind is by graduating with a Ph.D.

In the U.S. there is a strong sense that university education proper is postgraduate, with a master's degree, however good, not in itself a guarantee of real academic worth. Indeed there is a still growing differentiation in some of the most distinguished universities between the 'terminal' master's degree and one which is 'on the way' to a doctorate. In the American tradition there is much less attempt than in the British to identify an intellectual élite as such. The aim rather is to train and underwrite a professional élite—made up of those able to serve the academic, industrial and perhaps increasingly the administrative worlds with guaranteed competence. But this tradition, originally stemming from a thoroughly democratic impulse, is one which can be very confining and even deadening to the mind. Research pursued with intensity and a narrow concentration over five or six years is apt to diminish rather than increase contemplative capacity—directing the mind instead along paths which for many go through a more barren landscape than any they had bargained for, even with the hope of a crock-of-gold job at the end of the journey.

The explanation of the lack of desire in the U.S. to identify in the English way either a social or an intellectual élite is no doubt to be sought in the anti-aristocratic strands present in United States society generally and the strong tendency to make a proved capacity for maintained, reliable hard work a considerably greater social asset than cleverness. Normality is respected; to get the reputation for being an egg-head or a snob can be disastrous to one's advancement. One can graduate with a Ph.D. and escape some at least of the opprobrium of being classified as merely 'clever', for one has shown one's ability with resolution and in a solid way, and in the U.S. it is actuality and achievement that count.

During the decade 1960-70 the largest of the campuses of

the universities in the U.S. grew to the size of towns—the University of Minnesota at its Minneapolis campus, for example, by 1971 had 43 678 full-time students; the campuses of the University of California at Berkeley and Los Angeles over 27 500 each; the University of Michigan at Ann Arbor some 33 000.

No doubt the sheer size of the universities of which they were members was one factor in the movement of student revolt which between 1964 and 1970 itself was so conspicuous (and newsworthy) a feature of university life and of which more will be said in the next chapter. Emphasis should be laid, however, on four points in a movement which has, I believe, a good deal of significance for the future. First, that it was at Berkeley, one of the most lively of universities in the composition both of its faculty and its students, that it began in 1964; second, that the American example was one of the several factors influencing the rapid spread of open student protest (and violence) widely throughout the western world and helping to popularise it in countries influenced by the west; third, that, especially perhaps early in the movement, many very intelligent as well as articulate students were among the leaders; and fourth that the whole movement voiced an 'alienation' from what the students felt that civilisation, with the university as its instrument, was trying to do to them. However short-sighted, impractical, vengeful, and above all lacking in humility and self-judgement, many of those who took part in the demonstrations and riots (at such institutions as Columbia and Harvard as well as at Santa Barbara and Kent State) may have been, their motivation included among its elements a profound protest against the manipulation of men by a society which had come to think of education as important chiefly for its usefulness; not as concerned with maintaining or enhancing the humanity of human beings so much as making them efficient instruments of purposes whose long-term consequences no one really knew but whose short-term consequences were the production and marketing of more goods for private profit or national prestige and power.

It was this same decade 1960–70 which saw the rise in the U.S., for the first time anywhere, of a serious and maintained study of higher education itself as a phenomenon and social process. Since in the U.S. a far greater proportion of young people were coming to have a period of full-time higher education, a considerable amount of the research done and of the analyses made was of potential value to other countries if the right inferences could be drawn, for virtually every country during this time was expanding its higher education system at speed and planning to extend it further.

Of the hundreds of books written about higher education during these ten years, many of them drawing upon more dependable statistics and upon investigations carried out with improving instrumentation and gradually increasing subtlety, I would pick out four for special mention, two large-scale works, though not unconcentrated, and two much smaller ones, in a number of ways representative of the best thinking of the decade in this field.

The first of the seminal larger works is the distinguished anthology of essays *The American College* edited by Nevitt Sanford (1962). This is given unity by its perspective—at once sociological and humane—and the sureness with which it diagnoses the dilemma in which American (and by implication British) higher education was about to find itself: the confusion of purpose as between goals of social and personal development reflecting the conflict between the two in American life and indeed twentieth-century life generally. Yet this book is not philosophic in its main interest and intent; nor are the other three. The American strength in the examination of higher education is not philosophic but sociological, psychological, administrative, and it is increasingly aware as the decade goes on of economic factors which are highly influential and must be brought into the reckoning.

The other large-scale work is *The Academic Revolution* by Christopher Jencks and David Riesman (1968). This emphasises and documents the way in which American universities have been transformed into centres of professionalism and of efficient professionalisation—'colleague-oriented rather than client-oriented' (p. 201). It is the movement in this direction which constitutes the academic revolution. Against it the campaign for general education pursued between 1930 and 1960 by varied methods—at Chicago, Annapolis, Monteith, Bard, Harvard itself—has had little success, being in most cases simply 'taken over' by the professionalists. And the academic profession attaches little weight to knowledge derived from individual subjective experience.

Perhaps more immediate in its impact than either the Sanford or the Jencks and Riesman volumes has been Clark Kerr's short but highly concentrated *The Uses of the University* (1963) in which he coined the term 'multiversity', now so widely adopted as a term that captures at once the size, miscellaneity, serviceability, lack of unity and technical bias of the large contemporary university.

Less well known than the others is Carl Kaysen's succinct *The Higher Learning, the Universities and the Public* (1969). This argues pointedly that during recent years the cost of research has grown enormously. Its growth and the growth in overall size of the universities has outstripped private resources and is forcing them to rely increasingly on federal funds. But the new knowledge the state is willing to pay for is utilitarian knowledge; and in the period of retrenchment which is now upon us it may well find that universities are not the best places for such investment. For so far no rationale for continued public support of science and learning combines the virtues of intellectual validity and popular appeal. It is, Dr Kaysen argues, the college, not the university, that is the right place in which to give the kind of general education the undergraduate needs and for certifying that he has achieved the necessary standards for a first degree. The real job of the universities themselves is to cater appropriately for postgraduate work—but this, says Kaysen, significantly, should teach them not only how to research but how to apply their knowledge to difficult social problems. (He might have added that it is even more important to get them to see what the profoundest social problems really are.) Both colleges and universities ought, in essence, to be allowed to become once more primarily educative in their functions, instead of being producers of utilitarian knowledge with a pay off.

Corresponding to the movement during the 1960s in England to create some new universities and colleges which would break with an over-specialised approach to knowledge, a number of pioneer institutions of higher education were created in the U.S. which were experimental in character, normally on rural sites and often in the form of 'cluster colleges'. Among them were for example the University of California's campus at Santa Cruz (1965), the University of the Pacific (1961), Oakland College in Michigan (1965), Florida Presbyterian College at St Petersburg (1960) and Hampshire College in Massachusetts (1969). Most of them featured a curriculum which was in ingenious, often pioneering, ways 'interdisciplinary'—a term which in itself can of course mean many different things. Their significance lies not merely in the protest against the orthodox which they voice but their determination to work out a diversity of actual programmes which they could believe in. In this way they could act to some extent as laboratories for universities and colleges that were not in a position to be so bold. It would be easy, however, to over-estimate the extent to which such non-conformist institutions could convert ones that for a hundred good reasons had to be more conformist. Among those reasons the non-availability of sufficient new finance for change, though real enough, was probably not among the most important. Still more influential was the unconscious conviction within many minds that the prevailing economic and social outlook was essentially right. The minds concerned included those of many within state legislatures, of many trustees of universities, of alumni, parents and members of staff. They did not include the minds of quite a number of students.

Chapter 4

Changing Student Attitudes: The Significance of the Later Sixties

Student protest has of course a long history in countries where economic, political or religious oppression has threatened volatile youth. But the western movement of student disaffection whose onset was marked by the Berkeley revolts of 1964 and 1965 has been followed by bitter protests, sometimes violent, sometimes non-violent, in Paris, Tokyo, London, Berlin, New York and many other university cities. Though a period of quiescence has followed there is little evidence and no confidence on the part of far-sighted people that the fundamental sources of the disquiet have been removed. No doubt some of the revolts between 1964 and 1970 were simply a following of 'what is done' in an age when news travels fast. Moreover, violent action has a violent interest as well as its own publicity value for participants both as individuals and groups. The causes of student rebellion have been different in different countries; in some party political elements have been important factors. But there are many indications that the alienation of student opinion manifested so dramatically in the later 60s has sprung from causes deeper than a following of fashion or quick seizing of political opportunity. The movement had within it an element of profound protest against much of what had been taken for granted in higher education and in society generally over many years. It represented what Martin Trow (1972) has called the breakdown of consensus:

'Relations between professors and students no longer can be built on a broad set of shared assumptions, but are increasingly uncertain and a source of continual strain and conflict. Large parts of the university are still insulated from the sharpest experience of these conflicts . . . But every year more academic men experience at first hand the corrosive effects of ideological controversy . . . On the one hand, we see a traditional view of the liberal university, committed to teaching, research, and a variety of "services" to other institutions, but with sharp limits on its permissible intervention as an institution into the political life of the environing society; on the other, a profound hostility to that society and a passionate belief that the university is, or ought to be, a major instrument for its reform and transformation.

'We cannot be sure whether these attitudes and views of young academics will persist and transform the institutions, or whether they will be transformed by time and the power of the institution. Nevertheless, I tend to believe that the differences that we are finding are not likely to disappear over time, but are likely to persist and perhaps become sharper' (pp. 67-8).

When there is much thrashing about, mist and spray, it may be difficult to locate the centre of a disturbance. Nor can it be assumed that students, biased by the emphases of the education they have received before entering a university and by the type of society in which they have been brought up, are always going to be balanced in their diagnosis of what is wrong. They may easily mistake what the remedies are, even if remedies exist. But that they were sure that they were not and are not getting from their higher education what they hoped it would give them: this was, and is still, apparent enough. So is their latent distrust of society.

It may be pointed out that students in the later 60s had far more freedom than students fifty years before, though their predecessors then may not have noticed that they lacked it. Students half a century ago protested less; they fitted in, by and large, with the social requirements and the social goals of adults. There may have been rags and practical jokes, but they were only superficially discontented. For in fact they lived inside an accepted social order which was carried along by convictions and purposes that were less under question. The slack tides of our own time are more permissive. What students in the 1960s who felt they needed freedom may really have been needing most was a life that had a direction that seemed worthwhile, instead of finding themselves drifting along, 'the sport of every random gust'. They may have been, almost without knowing it, feeling deprived of meaning in life and in their studies. Ought not places of higher education, more than any others indeed, to be places today in which questions about objectives both in education and social life may properly be asked and a *raison d'être* for living properly be found?

Some of these underlying reasons for student malaise were brought out in some detail by the Report, never well enough known, of the Study Commission on University Governance (1968) issued from Berkeley.

'One major source of our troubles', it says, 'is found in the uncertainty and scepticism concerning the proper relations of the university and society. In the past, a reciprocity existed between them which found society willing to extend economic support to higher education in exchange for useful knowledge and trained personnel. That relationship was based on the principle that the existing organization of society not only would allow university graduates to contribute their skills in ways that would be socially useful and personally satisfying, but that the broad goals of society were such as to command general approval. As long as that situation prevailed, it was possible for students to view with equanimity an education aimed at preparation for specified careers. Now, however, they are increasingly critical of the world and of the institutions which shape it. Some of the most thoughtful and serious students have come to repudiate many of the social goals and values they are asked to serve in the university and upon graduation. That repudiation is directed in part at the conditions of technological society which seem to threaten human dignity. The new world emerging seems to exact greater conformity, more routinized lives, more formalized relationships among individuals, and a deeper sense of helplessness amidst an increasingly abstract world devoid of human values.

'This repudiation could be interpreted as the esthetic posture of traditional collegiate disillusion were it not for the growing belief, by no means confined to students, that contemporary society is afflicted with grave problems which it cannot solve and which can only worsen. Racial conflicts have become so intense that conventional solutions seem superficial; the ugliness and squalor of cities seem beyond repair and fit only for the violence which erupts in their streets; the skies are fouled and the land and forest ravaged; above all, the republic seems hopelessly entangled in a nightmare of a war with ever-widening circles of suffering, destruction and cynicism. Faced with this crisis, many students express intense dissatisfaction with the university since it provides much of the knowledge and most of the trained personnel required by the technological and scientific society. The university is, as one economist put it, a vital part of "the knowledge industry" and thus it contributes in important ways to shaping society in forms which evoke neither respect nor affection. It is little wonder, then, that many students are no longer willing to spend their college years preparing to "take their places" in such a society. Nor is it surprising that many students regard as irrelevant the miscellany of superficial, uncertain choices and professional training which often passes as the curriculum.

'Such discontent with the university is deepened by the degree to which the university's atmosphere reproduces the characteristics of the society. The university is large, impersonal, and bureaucratic. The acquisition of specialized skills has often been substituted for the education of persons, instead of supplementing it. Some of the most marvellous

51

expressions of human dignity—the activities of learning, inquiring, and sharing which are brought together in education—are being dehumanized. "Instruction" tends to usurp the place of inquiry; specialized "training" gradually commences at ever earlier stages of education; and the tempo of education is stepped up to meet the pressure of enrollment, the resentment of taxpayers, and the competition with other technological societies for national supremacy in the space age. The result is that instead of the warmth and cordiality which are the natural accompaniments of learning, relationships tend to be remote, fugitive, and vaguely sullen' (pp. 8-9).

Many when this was issued thought that it went too far, and Europeans anyway could say that it reflected an American situation rather than one nearer home. But the prevailing winds blow from the west; the influences of the mass media, of cut-throat commerce, rapid travel, a detached bureaucratic government, lack of moral conviction, are influences affecting —and increasingly so—very many countries. What makes the U.S. interesting and significant for us is partly the magnification and clarity with which things happen there. As the scale of the American landscape is bigger than the British, and for the most part the European, so the American dilemma is in certain respects our own writ large.

The apparent demand of student protests, whether about more important or less important issues, and whether in France, Spain, Germany, Britain or the United States, may well have seemed to be for 'freedom from' this or that confinement or condition, as if such an objective was itself the goal. A mere absence of constraints, however, can easily lead to unbearable confusion. Few people in fact can do with more than a limited quantity of lawlessness. But how does a society come by morality or by principles at a time like ours? They can neither be invented nor taken over second hand. They come from having roots, from sources which may start by being unconscious, but that lead on to objectives, which, if they are to be attained, must be brought up into consciousness and examined rationally.

Students themselves pointed out (more loudly in 1968 than in the early 1970s but with no essential withdrawal today from the same position): 'Our society is in a mess and it is older people, not we ourselves, who are responsible for that mess. We simply find ourselves in it. In modern conditions pressures and propaganda are subtle; if we are to argue in a rational way, we need to break with the older generation completely. Trading out must precede any trading in. We suspect the over-30s as having a design on us; we suspect the regulations liked or imposed by administrators; compulsions of many sorts; pomp and ceremony of many kinds; the wearing of gowns, stately university processions, degree givings, dignified and cold architecture. We want freedom from pressures so as to give us a chance to feel and think for ourselves. If sometimes there has been violence in the way we sought our ends, there is also a violence in the *status quo*; its compulsions are no less of an outrage because so many take for granted the presuppositions whether of capitalism or communism, of Christianity or humanism. We do not want to be graded by examinations into A's or B's or C's or First, Second and Third class categories. A plain pass or fail arrangement, if you please, preferably arrived at by continuous assessment: it is more democratic, less unjust, less a test of mere performance, making inequality still more unequal.'

The retort to such propositions might be: 'In practice the difference between the generations can easily be exaggerated. In fact, it is not simply the older generation still alive which is responsible for the mess but also, to some extent, the previous one, the one before that, the one before that again, and so on. There is at least some possibility that the younger generation will in due course itself be blamed in turn. Some humility, mixed with a lot of resolution, might not be a bad recipe. Are you willing to have your own grants cut for the sake of the cause you happen to be supporting just now, or is it always somebody else who is to carry the can? It is not difficult to find

scapegoats on whom to project relatively thoughtless dis-
contents—certainly much easier than to see and feel ourselves
as part, not merely victims, of the mess and already to some
extent responsible for it.'

Granted that University Councils, Trustees, Presidents or
Vice-Chancellors, professors and teachers in higher education
have much to answer for; that pressures towards conformity
are often subtle and can prevent a proper and desirable growth
of critical spirit—it still remains true that freedom to think is
not the same thing as thinking. It is possible to confuse a
passionate proclamation of one's rights with having deep and
well-thought-out principles. It is at least as easy for students to
be intellectually shallow as it is for dons. There are occasions
when forthrightness in speaking becomes a rationalisation for
hostility, when telling the real truth about things degenerates
into calling a spade a bloody Establishment shovel. Is there not
a kernel of truth in the notion that the honest man is one who
can quietly admit to this human tendency—and who, having
recognised it in himself, makes an honest effort to control it?
It would certainly be possible to arrange examinations on a
straight pass/fail basis, and there may well be a case for using
continuous assessment methods in all universities as they already
are in some. What one may have to consider, though, is
whether grading done as accurately as possible is or is not
justified in relation to other factors than the examinee's own
comfort. Is it or is it not useful in sorting people out for careers
or postgraduate studies? Does it help in giving them a more
accurate self-image, enabling them to face facts about themselves which otherwise they would not face? It is possible that
there are as many people surprised and encouraged by getting
a First or an A, as are surprised and discouraged by getting a
Third or a D. Is it the abler (or more hard-working) students
who suspect examinations or the less able (or less hard-
working)? How much do escapist or sentimental motives
activate the wish for a change? If every sort of classification of
degrees was abolished, the chances are perhaps that more
weight than ever would be given to the particular university

awarding degrees: to go to Oxford or Cambridge, Harvard or Princeton, might yield more than ever an unearned increment.

But it would be blind not to see that the more searching demands of students are too basic to be so easily answered. In some of them there is a self-forgetfulness, a commitment and conviction that go deep. One of the main objections to the *status quo* of those eager for progress is simply its deadness: its heavy, unreasoning opposition to change. If the *status quo* is defended by a faith which reasons, if it is prepared to evolve, to meet rationally the points put to it, it is at least alive. But it does not follow simply because one is young and *feels* free that one actually is so: the young can be and often are mentally as much in a condition of slavery as anybody; whether they are anarchists, hippies, or supporters of the establishment.

For younger and older alike, having freedom means having and using the chance to develop convictions to be tested by as much of the evidence as can be shown. To do so will mean making decisions of one's own—not giving in to pressure. This may of course entail the accusation that one no longer is identified with 'student opinion'; having to keep up with 'student opinion' may seem to some after a few years to be almost as much a tyranny as keeping up with any other. Making a free choice and keeping to it may include the willing acceptance of rules which when looked at coolly and objectively appear very like other rules. The rules personally acknowledged and kept seem and indeed are different from those obeyed as external demands.

The enthusiasm of the young may even at times be necessary to rescue the middle-aged from what Charles Carter has called the state of 'incorruptible indecision' into which they are apt to fall: a capacity for seeing what needs doing is one of the assets of youth from which age not merely should, but eventually has to, learn. Students may be the only likely source of initiative for some much needed changes in university outlook. There is without doubt a need for dons to be open to learn from their undergraduate contemporaries. As Jencks and Riesman (1968) say so perspicaciously, 'We do not see how adults can indefinitely contain the generational revolt. In the long run, undergraduates are almost certain to win increasing autonomy', though, as they admit, 'lacking a deep stake in the future of the community as a whole students may sometimes have a disproportionate interest in their civil liberties as against their civic responsibilities' (p. 57).

Many students, militant or quiescent, as we have seen, look upon contemporary life as lacking point. They are alienated from much of it, yet they are in no doubt that as students they are important, for civilisation simply cannot get on without the trained and thoughtful experts they are being groomed to be. The reaction of some may be to shout: 'Listen to us, will you? You are all manipulators; well, you aren't going to manipulate us.' But there are many for whom, whether they are drug takers or not, life today has become, in Northrop Frye's words (1969), 'a discontinuous sequence of immediate experiences' (p. 40). That is the case with many older people too, but they do not blame the university for such a state of affairs.

University students, however, at bottom have some hope that their place of learning can do something about the situation. Often it is the younger members of a university, both students and those who have recently become members of staff, who see most clearly the deficiencies of the relationship of institutions of higher learning to the world outside. The passions for (*inter alia*) equality, the rights of those they consider oppressed—whether the small nations or the workers —or for justice to coloured people, for relevant curricula and more social research whose outcome can directly contribute to the solution of national or local problems, carry a message which must be heard.

It is not really hard to envisage a society in the fairly near future in which people could be mere attendants of a technical apparatus over which they have little control and whose purposes do not seem to be any of their business. It almost might seem as though students have begun to be half aware of the danger that humanity might become a race of dwarfs—

leading dwarfs and following dwarfs, inventive dwarfs and non-inventive ones, but little men all the same. They might almost be remembering the speech which Brecht (trans. 1960) put into the mouth of Galileo in his play of that name: 'With time you may discover all that is to be discovered, and your progress will only be a progression away from mankind. The gulf between you and them can one day become so great that your cry of jubilation over some new achievement may be answered by a universal cry of horror' (p. 118). Some students and young teachers of science and applied science are now among the most convinced of the need to discover relevant ways of safeguarding their techniques from the de-humanising which may result from blindly applying them.

The permissiveness of which we spoke earlier can perhaps be seen as a demand, however excessive, for people to be given a chance to achieve kinds of learning that cannot be got except from a shared situation. One of the marks of contemporary student policy is not only increased unionisation, but a new recognition of kinship with other students—whether in Britain they are in polytechnics, colleges of education or other universities; whether in the United States they are in private universities, public ones, state colleges, liberal arts colleges. Clearly the British National Union of Students and America's Students for a Democratic Society have a very different self-image and a very different degree of confidence from those they had only a few years ago, and student attitudes and movements tend to be increasingly international in character.

Long ago Plato remarked that a change in the laws of music preceded a change in the laws of the state. Whether both are outcomes of the change in social climate or whether one leads on to the other may be a moot point. But that there is a relationship seems probable. A movement of mind so wide-spread and potent outside formal education, and obvious in the arts, music, architecture and many other expressions of human creativity, is more than likely—if it continues—to have its influence inside. A change of direction of interest, of heart and of desired life-style as international, affecting as many young

c

people, as the one we have been talking about, is a significant phenomenon; the protest within it goes deep. The movement is likely powerfully to influence curricula, concepts of the nature of general education and methods of teaching.

It may be that we are re-discovering some parts of our human nature recognised earlier in history, but forgotten or overlooked these last 150, even 300, years. There are numerous causes for this. Among them is an awakening suspicion, justifiable or not, of the rationalising capacities of the mind. The new mood is apt to suspect too wide an application of 'the unbridled lucidity' of the scientific attitude itself, indispensable though that attitude is to human progress. A profound questioning of the moral values of their own society implied in the criticism by American students of the Vietnam war was one of the earlier elements within the making of this counter-culture. But in its reaction against putting too much weight upon the analytic mode it has its counterparts in many other countries. In Sweden, Germany, Holland, France, Japan, Britain, there is a deep questioning of familiar and traditional institutions. There is a demand for more openness and spontaneity. Action itself has seemed to some to have unchallengeable authenticity.

The whole direction of movement no doubt owes a debt to Goethe, to Blake, to Nietzsche, to the German and French existentialists, especially Camus, and to Freud. More recently contributors to the stream have included Erikson, Polanyi, Maslow, Marcuse and Susanne Langer, together with such younger writers as Friedenberg, Roszak and Chomsky. For them teaching has the character of a transaction rather than a transmission of fact or truth from older to younger. But philosophically the movement is as yet confused. It has little use for history or for the past at all, and its concept of the moral is primitive. Only a morality grounded in some more rational and permanent order than the existential present is strong enough to support an ethic of openness.[1]

The really important consequences for higher education of

1 Cf. *The Sciences, the Humanities and the Technological Threat.*

the powerful new emphasis on the subjective and the personal are not of course likely to lie in the establishment of badly organised, so-called Free Universities—mis-titled, evanescent, inadequate in premises and staffing, and lacking intellectual standards. The significance lies much more, first, in the fillip which is being given in orthodox universities around the world to the arts and social sciences with more students looking to them with hope; second in the new incentive and confidence provided for the humanities to work out a discipline which is really theirs instead of one taken over from the sciences; and third in the new opportunity for developing courses that are a more meaningful combination of studies than the somewhat casual miscellanies often called 'interdisciplinary'. The idea that specialist studies must be the core around which liberal studies are grouped has become acceptable; the difficulty is to find teachers who know enough to cut the necessary channels and are able to reveal themselves as human beings with enthusiasms for ethics, philosophy or for one or more of the arts, open yet disciplined of mind.

Alan Harwood, who recently conducted for the Carnegie Corporation an inquiry into how the medical education of undergraduates could be better related to the human needs of the patient, reported that there were in his view two 'teachable moments' in the life of the medical student—one during his first year of medical school; the other at the start of his clinical years. By then he has in most cases become 'scientised' and tends to look at a patient as a mass of symptoms. The change to a new educational setting provided a good opportunity to introduce a new view of the patient as a total human being.

Am I right in thinking that the beginnings are visible of a significant new emphasis on the experiential? Of recent years the development on a large scale of American campuses and programmes overseas (the University of California alone has Directors of Studies in fifteen countries in four continents); the encouragement both in Britain and the United States of young people to spend a year between school and college in some voluntary or paid work; the adoption in British technological universities and polytechnics of the sandwich principle; the slowly increasing acceptance of the practice of music, creative writing, drama, art and first-hand criticism as optional if not compulsory contributions to degrees are all examples of a change of concept of what is proper within or in relation to an undergraduate course. In a later chapter we shall have more to say of the significance of such broadening. But the very emergence of a different emphasis, a different concept, trains a searchlight on the central problem facing our universities now.

Chapter 5

The Central Problem

The problems facing higher education at the start of the 1970s are obviously very great and very many. But essentially they stem from the difficulty of educating young people brought up in a society so uncertain and confused as ours about its own objectives, at a time when an enormous increase in our technical accomplishment and control over nature and human nature has occurred. Any solution demands a moral insight and moral choices that are products of a profoundly humane temper, one very different from that likely to be produced by an education directed to the production of technical skills, however complex and demanding of intelligence.

For example, with the perfecting or near perfecting of contraceptive devices for men and women—and the availability of abortion in case of 'mistakes'—a different situation presents itself from the one which has hitherto obtained. One can react by playing down the importance or significance of sexual experience, marriage and the family. But that involves risks of enfeebling sources of value and of principle which are parts of the heritage of western civilisation. Maybe we can dry up such sources and do without them. But we have few substitutes for them likely to be as good or ones that enable us to face as many of the facts about human love, responsibility and mortality. There is a certain lack of depth and imagination in some of the advocates of every kind of sexual freedom which makes one wonder if they are not already influenced by a technological manipulative frame of mind, far more escapist than they are aware of.

Another example comes from the power which technological knowledge seems to be about to put into men's hands of breeding future human beings with close control over their inherent capacities, intelligence, even temperament. Cloning—that is the breeding of a whole sequence of absolutely identical beings—has already proved possible in the case of frogs. It may or may not ever be possible in the case of men, but whatever the degree of exactitude with which we can choose the sort of people we want to have peopling the earth a nearer approach to it is fearsomely likely. This leaves us with some extremely difficult choices to make: What kinds of human beings *are* most human? How important do we really think a cold analytical intelligence to be relative to kindness, understanding and capacity for affection? The more fundamental the choices which technology puts it within our power to make, the more important imaginative insight and foresight become, and the more important is moral judgement. But such qualities and capacities are not of a technical kind; they are themselves the attributes of human beings, not of automata. They may perhaps be developed by education, including tertiary education, though primary and secondary education may well be more important. What is certain is that they cannot simply be created without a perception—not itself technological in nature—that they are desirable and humane.

Again, there is the application of technological knowledge to control the size of the world's population or of the population of any part of the world. It is agreed already on all hands that we cannot go on indefinitely, or indeed for much longer, allowing the peoples of the earth to grow in number at anything like their present rate. But on what principles should we limit the proportions of black, brown, white and yellow? Should we seek to stabilise world population at its present size? the number alive fifty years ago? or the probable numbers fifty years hence? The kind of judgement called for is not one to be made simply according to food supply, the number it is possible at maximum to support with the amount of nourishment attainable or theoretically obtainable. Questions of standards of living are involved, and not material standards only. The question of what human life is *for* is not far off. That is not a technological question but one with philosophical, moral and religious elements in it.

Clearly, a type of higher education which concentrates on the production of technological men is not in itself sufficient; it grows less and less so the more advanced our technological knowledge becomes. It is not contended that we can, or could possibly, educate a generation of people who will know definitively or in detail the answers to these particular problems or to the many others facing us. What is contended is that any adequate form of tertiary education should awaken minds to a realisation that more mastery of a technical sort will not in itself solve them for us. It is not enough even to equip men and women to be well informed in general, experts in one or more special fields, tolerant, lucid in argument and able to apply their knowledge. What of capacity for personal experience? for personal recognition of moral authority? for facing the fact of human finiteness? If we simply say that it is not the business of the college or the university to be concerned with such things we are trading out of the real situation; as we are if we maintain that the only source of authority is logical deduction from observed facts. This is to perpetuate if not enhance the impoverishment of the authority of reason itself, only one of whose main criteria, as we saw in Chapter 1, is of this type. An understanding of the kind of authority which has personal roots as well as that which is more impersonal is emphatically something which a higher education should be concerned to produce. That, however, means turning a corner in our whole concept of higher education. It may be that higher, as distinct from further, education cannot long survive unless we do turn this corner—and face the practical consequences involved.

The fact is that higher education has to become a lot more responsible than it has been, both socially and personally. We have not, I think, by any means as yet realised the extent of the revolution required in the next fifty years to make it so: the changes of assumption that are called for, the changes of orientation, the changes of content.

The basis on which so much of the content of higher education has so far rested is that personal experiences and social values are not as real or in the last resort as important as physical entities, hard facts and verifiable laws—the facts of history and of petrology; of physiology and of linguistics; the laws of mathematical reasoning and of climatology. A strict detachment and neutrality, we have argued, and argued logically, are indispensable if we are to understand the world and eventually perhaps the universe itself, with personal hopes and desires discounted—at times, it may be, heroically. The search therefore has been for an empirical method free as far as may be possible from feelings, biases, presuppositions. If the whole truth can never be discovered, at least this is the way patiently and gradually to find out more and more of it: it would be stupid and self-deceptive to imagine that there are other reliable routes.

I do not for a moment doubt that approaches to knowledge through experiment, theorem and deduction must be continued—and continued with energy and resolution. But by themselves they are not enough. If we lose the capacity for learning of a more directly 'felt' experiential kind we shall sacrifice more than we can possibly afford. We shall deplete our humanity. In such circumstances, higher education can and will betray us.

What must be emphasised is that the approach to knowledge through experiment and deduction itself involves a number of assumptions—for instance that it is possible to be detached without having made presuppositions; that 'facts' can be isolated from experiences. But we depend in all our perception or testing of fact—both mathematical and scientific fact—upon the ways in which we apprehend time, space and sequence. There is an element of interpretation in our observation of every phenomenon. Even in our ways of isolating phenomena from one another we depend upon common human traditions in feeling, sensing and interpreting. We separate out the act of observing and examining an entity from the act of imagining what it might be like to be that entity—dividing the physical from the animal, and the animal from the human, worlds. But we do this at least in part for convenience, not because the nature of things causes us to do so. In deducing and creating a theory about the laws of the physical world a scientist looks at his electrons from an external viewpoint. He assumes that, at any rate for his purposes, they are all identical and from his detached examination they may be as nearly as can matter. But so, of course, may the individuals in a crowd of human creatures seem, especially if they are of a different colour and belong to a different race from ourselves. What is more significant, however, is that in the case of human beings we do not confuse them clinically, as physiological or even psycho-analytic specimens, with knowing them as friends, knowing what it feels like to be them, realising something of their uniqueness as individuals, different from ourselves but in a measure understandable because we know something of what it is like to be us. The assumption that every sheep or every cell or every electron is 'the same' as every other may be totally justifiable for certain purposes; but nonetheless it remains an assumption.

An historian much more obviously relies both upon self-understanding and upon traditions in interpreting what happened in past situations. In imagining what took place in a particular case he makes use of his estimate of what is possible and probable in the natural order and in human nature. The view of the world which he has will in part determine what events in the past he notices at all, or takes to be significant. Victory, material prosperity, success, for example, he will normally estimate as more important and desirable than defeat and failure. Those who are daily engaged in the use of methods of history and science can be fully occupied without devoting a great deal of attention to the presuppositions they are using.

Sociologists and psychologists habitually rely upon a good

deal of understanding of themselves and their own way of reacting, or nearly reacting, to the world to secure data for their subject. It would be impossible to know anything *about* instincts, or repressions, or compensation, or social pressure, if no one knew from personal experience what these things meant or could mean. A text-book knowledge of such entities is only likely to be useful occasionally—for examination purposes, if those. To *understand* them we are dependent upon ability to understand ourselves and to go on thence to identify ourselves with other humans by a leap of sympathy. There are many assumptions concealed within such a process for all of us—for example that our own personalities are continuing realities; that the personalities of other people are in major ways like our own; that identity is a viable concept; and that people can be socialised and individualised in differing degrees. 'We have', says Professor George Woods (1965), 'no satisfactory images or concepts of the identity or continuity of the life of a personal being. But we have no persisting doubt of our own existence and we are not wholly without some notion of what it means to be, and to be an active personal being' (p. 8). It is this kind of fact with which most teachers in higher education have had few dealings, at any rate as teachers, and of which they have taken too little account.

It is because the world in which we live as persons is one in which we share common experiences that we can understand one another at all. We can observe and study our experiences; we can detach ourselves from them for particular purposes. But we are dependent upon them as men for interest, feeling, perception, individuality. It is impossible to live a life from the outside; to sense, to love, to value, to understand, depend upon capacity at least sometimes to be inside. To ensure on the one hand a strong awareness of the objectively measurable and its importance in our civilisation and to encourage on the other an awareness of one's own sensings, impulses, affections, insights, must be among the objects of a general education. 'A culture survives principally', as Philip Rieff (1966) has said, 'by the power of its institutions to bind and loose men in the conduct of their affairs with reasons which sink so deeply into the self that they become commonly and implicitly understood—with that understanding of which explicit belief and precise knowledge of externals would show outwardly like the tip of an iceberg.' It is easy to 'fail to take into account the degree of intimacy with which this comprehensive interior understanding . . . binds even the ignorants of a culture to a great chain of meaning' (pp. 2, 3).

The theory of knowledge which has been dominant in our time tends, as I have suggested, to take man's own capacity for experiencing, his feelings of his own significance, even his own sense of responsibility, too little into account. A psychology which speaks entirely in terms of 'behaviour', apart from its danger of treating human reactions only by reference to animal ones, can deprive us of even the possibility of actions that are moral. It counts them as irrelevant. A sociology which sees all social movements as outcomes of material or economic causes does not allow for our hopes of freedom, our workings of conscience, our feelings of responsibility. 'A human being, making a responsible decision and dedicating himself to action', says Michael Polanyi in *Education and the Nature of Man* (1967), 'can be understood only by responding to his situation as if it were one's own.' Systems of explanation which would avoid such involvement are defective. 'There is', he goes on, 'a hierarchy of levels in the universe . . . each higher level demanding a deeper participation for understanding it' and this offers hopes of a 'perspective in which we can once more place first things first. the living above the inanimate, man above the animal and the duties of man above man' (p. 15). Yet many teachers of the subjects in the higher education spectrum apparently seek a complete detachment from any personal involvement in life or situations. Nor do their systems of explanation necessitate such an involvement at any point.

How at this rate are we ever to come to a view which takes all the factors into account, including those insights, that love, that personal responsibility, which we sometimes undeniably feel? There is undoubtedly a disinclination in many academic circles to reckon with such feelings. Let us, it is said, stick to our lasts and talk of what we can observe and/or prove with some certainty. But if it is not the business of the thinkers and teachers in universities to attend to such matters, whose business is it? Moral judgements are implicit in many of the procedures and most of the policies we follow or agree to in the world outside. Such judgements need to be brought up into consciousness as far as may be. Does not an agricultural scientist who advocates the development of bigger and more economically run broiler houses base his advocacy upon a series of value judgements? The advocate of broiler houses can no doubt claim that by this means good cheap food can be provided, at a reasonable profit to the producer, for large numbers of people in our overpopulated world. But the feeding of multitudes at such a cost to the rights even of animals may well add to human moral insensitivity. To promote broiler houses because they produce more much-needed food does not end the responsibility of the agricultural scientist. He has solved, in part, one problem: that of feeding people. His method has created another: cruelty to chickens. He recognises this, probably, but condones the cruelty on grounds of the greater importance of people. He has not recognised the next resulting problem: the extra degree of de-humanisation and of desensitisation which will certainly result for some from habitual indulgence in a condoned cruelty. He must now face this next responsibility, which is to devise a non-cruel method of producing cheap chickens—one which does not deny the animals their rights. Instead of broiler birds we may almost unnoticingly go on to produce broiler men: indeed we may already be on the way to doing that. The general moral temperature may be lowered.

The experimental neurologist at work on his monkeys may cause them extreme suffering and degradation, but may be able to justify his usage of them by the hope that eventually human lives may be extended or relieved from almost unendurable pain. He will have to decide himself the way out of his moral dilemma. The very job of carrying out his experiments with monkeys day by day may tend to blunt his moral sense. Unless he is careful, human beings too may be used experimentally in a way which comes to seem to him as defensible as using monkeys. The distinguished American neurosurgeon, Irving S. Cooper (1969), writes: 'A few years ago during an international meeting of neurologists and neurosurgeons, an eminent professor, one of the most brilliant innovators in modern neurosurgery, in describing an operation which carried considerable risk and was extremely difficult for the patient to endure, said, "We do not advocate nor are we embarking on any therapeutic regime. It is an experiment". He then outlined the technical difficulties and dangers inherent in the procedure, concluding, "all of this cannot be thought of in any way as a therapeutic procedure". No one rose to argue that this type of procedure, performed on a human being by a surgeon who states that it is not a therapeutic procedure, is absurd' (p. 109).

The responsibilities of surgeons are not limited to performing their operations with as much compassion for the patient as possible nor to restoring him to health or sanity. In future more often than now surgeons and medical scientists will have to decide whether and when to transplant organs from one human being to another in order to improve his capacities or functioning. What 'improvement' can be effected in a man or woman without making them different in their identity from what they were before? What changes of personality may legitimately be brought about? And what are the limits of justification in such a matter? The more man gets control over his environment and takes charge of his own development the more his decisions must incorporate a moral element and the more important will be his concept of what attributes are most desirable in human beings. We may defend the growing of two blades of grass where one grew before, or the fattening up of pigs, or the addition of chemical preservatives to breakfast cereals, on the grounds of the increase to human prosperity and health that these policies may bring. But what is an 'improvement' in human evolution? Planners need to be more than manipulators: they need an understanding of what it really means to be man and to have values in control of the manipulation. Such values are not simply proclamations of goals or of ends but affect at every stage the choice of what means shall be used to attain them.

The educator may sometimes have to choose whether it is more important for students at a given time to add to their knowledge and technical skills or to their experiences—and what levels or quality of experience they may be most in need of. When we are told that research has shown that watching T.V. not merely adds greatly to knowledge but imparts a wider vocabulary and enables children to be more vicariously experienced, what are the criteria for determining whether the experiences are important or desirable? We are assured by Professor Hilde Himmelweit (1958) of the London School of Economics that 'children who watch T.V. develop a more objective response to many situations'. But is this a substitute for feeling themselves into a range of situations which it would be good for them to understand or chiefly an inoculation against manifestations of life which they would find insupportable if involved in them themselves? Research workers in education and psychology are themselves sometimes deficient and unpractised in these very sorts of insight and 'experiencing power'.

A distinction is to be drawn between knowledge which includes an understanding of feeling, loving, acts of valuing, and knowledge which is external, concerned with facts, measurement, the 'behaviour' of things. Both kinds are indispensable to a properly human and a properly humane life. The kind of personal and moral commitment which is the mark of the civilised man is not an irrationality. A sense of purpose that is intelligent includes an analytic and deductive exercise of mind but does not stop there.

By and large, universities today are much better at imparting knowledge and techniques that are what I have called 'external' than at fostering either aesthetic or moral awareness. They are more interested in training experts than experiencers. The university graduate rarely lacks a good deal of knowledge; he is more likely to lack an ability to find much meaning in life, to keep in touch with himself, or a sense that the past—even his own past—in any real sense belongs to him.

Most of the vast numbers of students entering higher education in Britain, the United States and many other countries, in the next quarter of a century will be looking to their period in a college or university or polytechnic to fit them for a profession or to give them expertise to equip them to survive in the technological world they will live in. Because money is limited, it is likely that more will be studying part-time. Staffing ratios will be lower, though more and cleverer devices to help their instruction will be available, so more of their education will be self-directed. In Britain, as we have seen, a large percentage of the extra students will go to polytechnics rather than to universities; more will be living at home rather than in colleges or halls or lodgings or flats. But in universities far too many of the courses we give are conventionally academic and unconsciously designed to transform the brighter by gradual stages into professors. And we have hoped that somehow this recipe will work for the rest as well. Such a programme is obviously inappropriate now and will become even more so as greater numbers of students crowd into higher education.

Yet the job of civilising and sensitising these students both morally and aesthetically will be the more imperative in a world becoming more adept year by year at making men into performers, consumers made contented only by more consumption, people able to gratify the maximum number of desires in a given period of time, but finally left at the mercy of their merciless instincts—like smaller modern Faustuses or Don Juans. And all in the name of progress.

What is the answer? Ought higher education to be in the least concerned with the challenge? One can of course declare that this is not an educational problem at all; or if an educational problem, one for churches, governments or political parties—anything rather than colleges and universities, whose task is to pursue knowledge through rational inquiry and to discipline reason in a narrower sense.

I do not believe that that is a realistic position in the period ahead. Something is wrong with our theory of knowledge if we divorce knowing from being in such a way. Detachment is for the sake of living—not an end in itself. And life in a barrel, even a well-padded one, on its way over Niagara has all too short a date. Higher education must not merely broaden a student's sense of social responsibility, arousing in the potential expert an interest in the social consequences of practising his expertise. We must meet the more far-reaching and far more difficult challenge of sending him back to first principles and getting him to consider what is worthwhile in life.

There is no one recipe that will be successful in more than a fraction of the cases. But the direction of effort must be to broaden that sense of social responsibility once it has been aroused. The chemist who becomes concerned with the problem of effluents, the farmer who becomes alarmed at the side effects of spraying crops, the builder made aware of the social consequence of high-rise blocks—these are still a long way from necessarily being interested in the good life in general, or the links between social and personal. But they are at least a bit closer to considering the key question: how do we know that something, that anything, is worthwhile? As soon as that point is reached, hope glimmers, though the glimmer can easily fade if there is nobody to fan it to flame. And so often the teacher of agriculture, or chemistry, or surgery, or business administration or building is not good at such fanning.

How do we know something is worthwhile? The answer always involves an act of experiencing and an act of recognising the significance of the experience. First, we have personal feelings; second, we become aware of the feelings; third, we judge their importance.

For many people, music, literature, a film, a personal betrayal, a sudden bereavement, the break up of a love affair, may bring experience, but they do not link these things with anything they regard as education. They believe that education is learning things for use. The problem of how to connect using with experiencing at a deep enough level is the primary educational problem. It is this problem that causes Ivan Illich to advocate deschooling; that we should abandon our schools and colleges altogether because they cheat us of life.

That may be a counsel of despair. But the alternative is almost as drastic. How do we get our students to recognise any authority other than finite knowledge: knowledge won as a result of carrying on a kind of offensive against an implacable world, knowledge retained with difficulty at least till the examination is over or the essay has been written? I do not want to underestimate the value of this kind of knowledge. One of the enormous benefits which technology brings is that though the world may be implacable, if you can get the mastery over just one small bit of it you can become implacable too. You can *do* something in a world where most people feel impotent. This important kind of knowledge is finite and demonstrable. Evidence exists for it, and it takes logic, determination and strenuousness to achieve and prove it. But, as I have argued, there is also the knowledge yielded by evaluating our personal experiences. Unless we can judge these experiences, we have no way of learning to value anything else.

Western civilisation is full of people like Martha in the gospel story, busily attending to what they think are their proper jobs, and it is supremely difficult to get our students of technology or management or even philosophy itself to stop attending to those jobs for a moment and listen (so that they discover what they already know). Yet such listening is one way to find meaning in things and therefore to be able to judge their worth. Most conventional kinds of study, whether of the sciences or the humanities, are associated with effort. They discount the relaxation indispensable to experiencing. Much that is essential in education, I would maintain, is not research-minded; it is concerned with the parts of life that technical study neatly avoids; personal suffering, personal happiness, good and evil, commitment, the mysterious, the inextricable mixture of human motives. *Hamlet, The Marriage of Figaro,*

Willa Cather's *Death Comes for the Archbishop*, Greek myth, the powerful sculpture of the Mayas—all are dense with meaning that awaits our understanding. How are we to become quiet enough, individual enough, to realise their meaning or our own need? I have no easy answer. But I believe, all the same, that the ultimate alternative may be the destruction or rebuilding of the college, the graduate school, higher education itself, as we know them. For to educate people to be experts in a world that no longer has any meaning is a kind of madness and may come to be recognised as the madness it is.

'We know the answers, all the answers.
It is the questions that we do not know.'[1]

And without putting the questions searchingly to ourselves, the answers will be illusory.

What is a consumer society for? What is progress in aid of? I suspect that it is these questions that we should, with a desperate urgency, be asking; and that unless we can ask them at a level of understanding that it takes imagination and humanity to reach, we cannot really answer them at all. We need both intellect and lively affection, both capacity to analyse and capacity to feel, if we are to find any answers that have lasting meaning.

1 Louis Macneice.

Chapter 6

What Higher Education can Learn from Preceding Stages

I

The extent of the transformation necessary in the higher education we provide is therefore immense. An evolution in men's outlook and evaluation is involved. But I am well aware that this will not come for the asking and that the education we give, or can give, the young at any stage is a function of the society that gives it. You cannot change dramatically the presuppositions or the content of the education which is given unless society wants, or almost wants, that to be done. All the same, something can be accomplished through education to propel a desirable movement forward. A wheel can be made to rotate by pressure exerted at the right angle on any part of its circumference, even though, if it is stiff on the axle, pressures at similar angles may be needed at other points too.

Our contention is that the central problem facing us is not technological in character but one of finding meaning at first hand. We cannot escape from living in an age of technology or escape from inheriting a technological future, even if we wished to do so—and we do not. Man must be equipped to cope with increasing, not decreasing, complexities as far as the eye can see ahead, including the physical problems of planning cities of 20 million inhabitants, and the moral problems of living in those cities with 19 999 999 other inhabitants. But such coping will fail if it is at the cost of fresh, unbidden, undeceived, personal knowledge that life itself is worthwhile—

and that involves seeing and thinking into parts at least of the human situation itself.

I do not believe that there is a possible way out of the impasse without retention and enhancement of sensibility: of the power to feel and its disciplined education. Normally, however, by the time the stage of tertiary education is reached we have dissipated in the young much of their potentiality here, while during the period of tertiary education itself almost all the emphasis is deliberately placed upon training the mind to function analytically. This is and will remain indispensable, but it is no substitute for a broader education. But what is usually called general education, which anyway has no high repute after the age of eighteen or so, is normally conceived as having as its first job that of widening the students' interest in *problems* or of relating their knowledge of their special subject to additional areas in which it can be applied. It is of course entirely to the good that engineers should be induced to consider the effects of their bridge-building or reservoir-making upon, say, village life in Northern Nigeria; that ethical problems concerning contraception, transplants, racial ghettos, should be thoughtfully and coherently discussed. All this is needed, but much more than this too if we are as human beings to find life more than an interval—as pleasant as it can be made—between birth and death; or if human evolution is to be more than a progress in substituting automata for men.

We may best put ourselves in a position to face so basic a challenge to our present notions about the content and the scope of higher education if we look first at the kind of education which desirably might have preceded the tertiary stage. Where do we go wrong? Why are so many students, and their teachers, so acceptant of their own amnesia and anaesthesia, and so little aware of what but for their own earlier education they might have been?

It is often agreed that the earliest stages of the education given in schools—at any rate in Britain—are among the most successful, whatever successful may mean. Here without any doubt the emphasis is upon nourishing and extending the child's capacity to experience within a framework of presuppositions that he can take for granted about the nature of his world. His capacity for learning seems to be closely related to his capacity for experiencing and many things are grist to this mill. Part of the main effort of the school is directed to preventing the child's desires to sense and wonder and explore from becoming silted up; and so the good primary school is a lively place with plenty of incentives provided for activity and enjoyment as well as for observation. Education at this stage is not seen by anybody as a purely intellectual process; it involves the learning of attitudes and the acceptance of value judgements taken on trust from others, re-inforced as they will often be found to be by personal experiences themselves. The importance of good relationships between taught and teachers is clear enough, a reliable affection being almost demonstrably one of the indispensables if all round development is to take place.

Children brought up without love, though supplied plentifully with instructions and rules, will, it is known, tend to behave as obedient or disobedient mechanisms, more as automata than fully human beings, taking in this way perhaps a subtle if unconscious vengeance against society. Obedience to rules administered by cold human beings simply as external commands seems to be destructive of personality; children need instead to feel rules as expressions of right intention and feelings towards them. The influence of a good primary school is in part an inward influence, organic, intimate. Its constraints are disciplines of a kind which treat people as individuals from a very early age.

The emphasis upon children's exercising their senses and imagination and upon their learning to coordinate limbs and muscles in expressing experiences through words, paint, mime or dance has in mind the idea that more than we know we are dependent all our lives upon our ability to perceive the world freshly. If the elementary power to experience vividly through the senses is lost, life becomes poorer and more shrivelled; but more than this—ingredients and attitudes necessary for later introspection and correct analysis of the world will be missing. At no time in life can any one else see for us or hear for us, though they can suggest to us fruitful ways of looking and listening.

It is very early in life that a child begins to learn for himself the sheer objectivity of objects, their separateness from himself and their unamenableness. He learns an attitude to such facts, how to comport himself with them. There is after all no contradicting a wall which hurts you when you bump into it. The desire of the baby to push and pull, to arrange objects, is very much part of early play. The play material it is so important for him to have is material from which he begins to learn both how to manipulate the world outside him and to learn also with his muscles, tacitly, about gravity and friction. Such internal learning goes hand in hand with external. He learns with increasing consciousness which movements he can cause to be subject to his own will and which he cannot. There is pleasure in control and in being able to dominate. Everyone who has watched a baby delightedly scattering a pile of bricks to the four winds will recognise that the impulse which moves him is powerful. So are the impulses for building, for patterning, for planning, which gradually develop. One of the lessons to be drawn from studying child development is that the growth of some abilities is dependent upon the growth of others. Many sorts of deprivation have long-term consequences.

That the development of some qualities is based on the establishment of others is well brought out by Erikson (1961). 'Hope, will, purpose and skill', he says, 'are the rudiments of virtue developed in childhood.' Fidelity is an adolescent virtue; love, care and wisdom are the central virtues of adulthood. 'In all their seeming discontinuity these qualities depend on each other; will cannot be trained until hope is secure, nor love become reciprocal until fidelity has proven reliable . . .' (pp. 150-1). As man 'transmits the rudiments of hope, will, purpose and skill, he imparts meaning to the child's bodily experiences; he conveys a logic much beyond the literal meaning of the words he teaches and he gradually outlines a particular world image and style of citizenship' (p. 159).

Young children are obviously in several senses 'nearer to nature' than older people. It is not until adolescence that most children develop any noteworthy capacities for introspection; nor do most before they are teenagers seek a philosophy of life of their own. But though the primary school child lives a relatively unexamined existence, according to a relatively unexamined morality, the examination of his life he will later be capable of making is probably dependent at any rate to some extent upon the range, scope and order of his living both in its connections with the outside world and its sensings and interior imaginings. How closely he is in touch with his own real views or even his own desires or can get into touch with them is a product of many factors.

Human nature is highly adaptable and no doubt there is a chance for some people to live temporarily as if they were children again. They thus may have a second opportunity of acquiring experiences, and therefore ingredients for good living, which they had missed. This indeed is the theory upon which much psycho-analytic treatment is based. What is often forgotten is that people are dependent at the tertiary stage of their education upon the quality of their experiencing, learning, observing and introspecting at previous stages. There may be no cure for deficiencies in these respects except through recapitulation in some form or other of earlier life. This seems generally true whether within a 'free' democracy, high in technological accomplishment, or in a less competitive or developed society where men may grow up much less individualised. Many of the basic psychological needs remain the same.

Of those who have written about the earlier stages of education, both in theory and practice, Wordsworth has been among those with most to say that is relevant and among the most neglected—perhaps because much of what he said (but not all) is said in verse, perhaps because his educational philosophy, though often profound, is not overt nor always consistent. At any rate he is practically never mentioned in text books on education, let alone higher education. In *The Prelude*, at the age of thirty or so, he looks back over his development and tries to set down the significant periods of his upbringing from early infancy to well after Cambridge days. He recalls and recounts the events of his childhood and youth which brought him experiences, and so seeks to trace the stages by which he arrived at the possession of an identity. He has in mind not only how self-unity is to be attained but how it is to be preserved through early and later maturity. Perhaps by loyalty to the insights brought by moments of fear and awe, joy, betrayal, despair:

> 'There is a dark
> Invisible workmanship that reconciles
> Discordant elements, and makes them move
> In one society. Ah me! that all
> The terrors, all the early miseries,
> Regrets, vexations, lassitudes, that all
> The thoughts and feelings which have been infus'd
> Into my mind, should ever have made up
> The calm existence that is mine when I
> Am worthy of myself!'

It is not irrelevant to our purpose to emphasise the importance of Wordworth's insights into the relation between experiencing and knowing. What students today understand by a 'sensate culture' is given in his teaching a profounder extension of meaning and rationale than perhaps anywhere else. Theodore Roszak (1972) has shown the relevance of Blake's radicalism to the student awareness today of the dangers in the de-humanising power of our civilisation, an awareness to which I referred in Chapter 1. Wordsworth's message has equal contemporary point. He held that there were three main stages of development: childhood, the period of sensing; youth, the period of feeling and increasing self-awareness; and maturity, the period of thought and self-identification.

The natural child is unconsciously receptive to a thousand sensations, some of them haunting. During adolescence consciousness is powerfully at work—coordinating, criticising and disciplining: youth is a period of self-examination, of introspection. And there is no way to manhood save by this route. Childhood and youth are moments, and permanent moments, of our lives. 'The child is father of the man' not merely chronologically but at every instant. There is an intimate connection between receptivity and creativeness; the man separated from any return to the child in him is separated from the springs of his own being. He may have developed that precise technical control of the mind which is the power to analyse, but if it is at the cost of his instinctive life his thoughts will be out-of-touch with much that matters. In a word he will be a dis-unified 'modern man', his thinking instrumental to purposes he may not at heart believe in.

The child in the true health of his mind has an immense capacity for turning events into experiences; and in Wordsworth's view the mind is literally built up, composed, created from the experiences it has.

> 'There was a boy; ye knew him well, ye cliffs
> And islands of Winander!—many a time,
> At evening, when the earliest stars began
> To move along the edges of the hills,
> Rising or setting, would he stand alone,
> Beneath the trees, or by the glimmering lake;
> And there, with fingers interwoven, both hands
> Pressed closely palm to palm and to his mouth
> Uplifted, he, as through an instrument,
> Blew mimic hootings to the silent owls,
> That they might answer him. And they would shout
> Across the watery vale, and shout again,
> Responsive to his call,—with quivering peals,
> And long halloos, and screams, and echoes loud
> Redoubled and redoubled; concourse wild
> Of jocund din! And, when there came a pause

Of silence such as baffled his best skill:
Then, sometimes, in that silence, while he hung
Listening, a gentle shock of mild surprise
Has carried far into his heart the voice
Of mountain-torrents; or the visible scene
Would enter unawares into his mind
With all its solemn imagery, its rocks,
Its woods, and that uncertain heaven received
Into the bosom of the steady lake.'

Here a creative experience is recorded; the setting down of a moment in the boy's life which had intense meaning for him. And the moment comes to the boy, alone, in the natural silence following the shouts; as it comes sometimes at a time of lonely fear. It was because of such experiences that Wordsworth in the *Immortality* Ode refers to the child as a 'Seer blest'. For Wordsworth imagination was another name for the power to experience, 'seeing into the life of things'. The awakening which such incidents brought about is, he believes, essential to the attainment of full maturity later on.

In childhood mind and heart work closely in unison. The darkness of the ground, the hugeness of the clouds or of great buildings in the city today, or of great diesel engines on the rail track or noisy, fast-moving cars, can have something of the elemental within them. The child spends a lot of his time in sheer activity, but there are minutes when he is spontaneously passive and absorbent. Such minutes tend to come in the tiny period of relaxation following some special effort or fear. There is a passage in De Quincey's *Literary Reminiscences* recording Wordsworth's statement: 'I have remarked from my earliest days, that if, under any circumstances, the attention is energetically braced up to an act of steady observation, or of steady expectation, then, if this intense condition of vigilance should suddenly relax, at that moment any beautiful, any impressive visual object or collection of objects, falling upon the eye, is carried to the heart with a power not known under other circumstances.'

The sort of knowledge which is important is not held in detachment: it is best thought of as being itself organic. It permeates the unconscious part of the mind; and of the importance of the unconscious Wordsworth was deeply persuaded long before later psychologists took it as their own discovery. Perhaps at the time of receiving an experience which sets up a creative disturbance in unconsciousness the child may be able to answer no questions about it. It is only at a later stage, and very likely not even then, that he will be able to point to a certain day and experience and know that then and there he was being 'educated', fashioned. Nevertheless it is such high moments which eventually make a person into an individual, an identity with his days 'bound each to each' by a 'piety' which can be the offspring only of feeling. Thus even a butterfly may become an 'historian of one's infancy', by bringing back to memory an experience of long ago.

But the influences to which Wordsworth looked for so much in their effect upon the child were not only a natural environment, with the beauty and awe and constancy, the stimulus to animal life and the opportunities for solitude and relaxation which that environment brought, but also human affection and companionship. He was glad that he himself had been introduced to simple-hearted countrymen and had not made first acquaintance with man in the unnatural environment of the town; man who had lost kinship with any small community; who was guarded and self-concerned; living in a realm of bustle and detachment from human concerns during business hours. Children were to be brought up among friends and away from crowded towns—where appeals to self-interest were visible at every turn. The shepherds and open-hearted Cumberland peasants whom Wordsworth knew in his childhood did not make the pursuit of money or of fame their goal. They were warm-hearted people; and to Wordsworth their warm-heartedness was in itself creative. It is not peculiar to country people but it is easily overlaid.

He defends the dame school because of the human, personal contact between the dame herself and the children. 'I will

back Shenstone's Schoolmistress by her winter fire and in her
summer garden seat', he says, 'against all Dr Bell's sour-
looking teachers in petticoats that I have ever seen.' Wordsworth condemned the infant schools of his day because they
separated children from their parents; and because they robbed
the child of many chances of affection, of feeling and experiencing. 'The bent of the public mind', he says in a letter
written to the Rev. H. J. Rose, 'is to sacrifice the greater for the
less—all that life and nature teach, to the little that can be
learnt from books and a master . . . Our course is to supplant
domestic attachments without the possibility of substituting
others more capacious. What can grow out of it but selfish-
ness? . . . Natural History is taught in infant schools by pictures
stuck up against walls and such mummery. A moment's
notice of a redbreast pecking by a winter's hearth is worth it
all.' He refers contemptuously to the plan by which children's
heads are stuffed with 'minute, remote or trifling facts in
geography, topography, chronology, etc., or acquisitions in
art or accomplishments which the child makes by rote and
which are quite beyond its age, things of no value in themselves but as they show cleverness'.

Wordsworth was as suspicious as Ivan Illich of any compul-
sion which would fill the child's time with book-study,
analytical exercises of various sorts and many facts to be
learned by heart. The product of real education, he thought,
was not scholarship or information so much as sympathy;
faith; moral insight; 'sovereignty within and peace at will'.

> 'Hence cheerfulness in every act of life, . . .
> Hence truth in moral judgements and delight
> That fails not in the external universe.'

Wordsworth foresaw with the coming of enforced education
an increase of self-concern and self-interest. The very possibility of maintained insight into what we should now call the
years of secondary and tertiary education, depended, he
thought, upon the existence of an imaginative life during

childhood and youth; and the stimulants of the life of the imagination are joys and pains which permeate the unconscious part of the mind—love of friends, personal suffering, a feeling for the mystery of things. The *Immortality* Ode is not engaged in establishing the doctrine of pre-existence, but the vividness and visionary quality of the experiences and memory of the child. If people are to retain coherence of mind, that is consistency in the values they set upon experience, they must not be forced and regimented by places of education organised to make them concentrate exclusively upon the training of the capacity to analyse and be put into over frequent friendless competition with others. Man cannot make adaptations with the speed of a machine; and if he is forced to do so, he will grow up superficial, unimaginative, insensitive. Wordsworth felt that the truths which matter are not those which come from strifeful seeking but those which 'wake to perish never'. In that word *wake* is contained a whole philosophy.

So much for the educative influences which Wordsworth thought necessary to the human development. But what products and results did he look for from them? In the first place he wanted early life to be lived so that a man might grow up with heart and mind not working against each other. Secondly, he wanted what might be called 'experienceability' preserved far into maturity. Too often during later adolescence sensitiveness and delight in sensing become lost; men become 'coated over'; and the capacity for vision and inward understanding diminishes. They become apathetic; and they make practicality the only or the final test. In the third place, he wanted kindness and the power of human sympathy to be preserved. Kindness he saw as an offspring of imaginative perception, and as itself an essential expression of individuality. Greetings without kindness and all the dreary intercourse of daily life are condemned.

In *The Excursion* Wordsworth re-emphasises the importance of the thread connecting childhood through the adolescent period with maturity. The poem is largely a record of the means by which mental health may be recovered in maturity when the natural path of development has been missed. If we have felt strongly in childhood and can be brought back into touch with the vivid sensings of those days, there is hope. For the spontaneous instinctive urges of the child become the feeling intellect of maturity. How indeed can we know what is normal save by reference to the spontaneous feelings of the child? 'In nature and the language of the sense' is still 'The anchor of one's purest thoughts, the nurse, The guide, the guardian of the heart and soul Of all the moral being.'

No doubt it is the reserved and introverted boy who is most fond of the savage grandeur of mountain scenery, finding in it symbols of his own longings. No doubt Wordsworth was living in an age when schools were far less likely to treat children as children than are schools today. But Wordsworth was not in himself a highly abnormal boy; and there is reason to think that such experiences as he had are the rule rather than the exception during the childhood of an imaginative and sensitive boy or girl whether brought up in town or country.

The central question of Wordsworth's reconsideration of his own childhood is this: how can people be helped to grow from the children they once were into men and women still, in and after university years, capable of creation, possessed of self-unity and 'the deep power of joy' when these are so easily lost? And in brief his answer is: they need the nourishment of inward life which comes through the availability of affection and friendship, of scenes and circumstances which are experience-bringing, which disturb the emotions, yet give chances for quietude and relaxation, which bring challenge and yet discipline the spirit by the fear they hold.

The reader may object—with some justification—that Wordsworth after all lived in an age when England, and most of all its Lake District, was still largely a rural country. It never will be again. Today young and old alike are town dwellers; places of higher education are sited in cities, with Oxford and Cambridge themselves victimised by industry. But essentially Wordsworth was emphasising to a simpler age and in a simpler environment a number of things which are inescapably true:

that analytic power is no substitute for awe; that what it really concerns a human being to know may change on the periphery but not at the centre; that if wonder becomes entirely subsidiary to achievement and power, de-humanisation is inevitable. The lessons he was concerned to teach are relevant enough; the methodology by which they can now be taught is different—and difficult.

II

It is certainly contended strongly and by the large majority that at the secondary and tertiary stages of education today the job is to prepare people for the late twentieth-century kind of world and the late twentieth-century kind of work upon which they will soon be entering. The argument is that effort should be concentrated chiefly upon giving them the kinds of intellectual and practical expertise they will need if they are to succeed in the kinds of competition their society approves. Relatively little attention should therefore be paid to subjects which are not conducive to this; and roughly speaking the more intelligent people are the more this should be so. The maintenance of sensibility is not at all an essential concern for institutions of secondary or tertiary education as their students grow from sixteen to twenty two. The temper of such places should become less that of communities, more that of places in which knowledge is being imparted for specific and definable purposes. It is unlikely that this will be entirely the case—especially in those schools or universities which because of their traditions, their coeducational nature, or the enthusiasms of particular people who happen to be members of their staffs, are more inclusive in the kind and scope of the education they give. But the prevailing tendency may well be towards a concentration on finite achievements, good passes in examinations for certificates, diplomas and degrees, and this will be the more powerfully so the greater the demand from society outside for labour that is intellectually alert and well equipped. The tendency may be further encouraged if the sixth forms and undergraduates are little known by anyone—even counsellors—as persons or as having moral problems, or in fact a life of any sort outside the institution.

Indeed, trained to distinguish between experiencing and education, the modern student is likely to regard any communication on a personal level with grown-ups as unnatural and any attempt on their part to 'understand' him as an intrusion. The most acceptable intermediary may be a counsellor or someone from the student health service who as it were is licensed as a professional to take note of some at least of his more personal needs. As they grow up, the modern adolescent and the undergraduate increasingly fit in with what contemporary society—almost without knowing it—requires of them. Society appears to want trained and successful participants in a largely industrialised and competitive world.

'Pre-occupation with individual test scores, though understandable in the individuals being tested, today I believe', says Edgar Friedenberg (1969), 'serves chiefly the ideological function of convincing the young that the American social system recognises and rewards individual competitive achievement . . . The major premise of the American system of social morality is that every individual should have an equal opportunity to compete for the prizes offered. The less frequently stated, but probably more crucial, minor premise is that, if he does, he has no other legitimate basis for complaint' (pp. 23, 28).

Entry to tertiary education in almost any country today may be almost purely a matter of satisfying certain technical requirements, the 'image' of a university or a college given to a boy or girl often being that of a place which is little interested in him except as a competitor with others. What kind of picture of one's possible future university or college would one get if one had to judge from their entry procedures, including in Britain the U.C.C.A. forms they have to fill in? Institutions of higher education are often unaware of the far-reaching consequences of their own entry requirements upon the curricula and attitudes of secondary schools. The matriculation examinations, the college entry tests which have to be passed at high level, concentrate on the measurable so that justice can appear to be done; we are too little aware even now of the bias built into them against abilities—aesthetic, practical, tender-minded—which do not fit neatly into conventional ideas of attainment and academic prowess.

In higher education, as in secondary and primary, penetrative teaching will still very much depend upon the understanding the teacher has of the student's shape of mind, his interests, his keennesses, his motivations, his sense of humour, his attention span—in a word, his personality. 'Adolescence is when you decide what you are going to be', said a boy of seventeen from Shoreditch to a friend of mine, speaking more profoundly than perhaps he knew. So often what causes a loss of the confidence that is indispensable for progress is that no one takes any interest in fostering the imaginative or intellectual powers of those between sixteen and twenty—of first-hand perception, initiative, originality, acumen in judging actual situations, sensitiveness. So often it is the act of recognition that is the creative one. Teachers and examiners are both normally much better at diagnosing and rewarding some kinds of ability than other kinds—which, because so little recognised, shrivel or remain undeveloped. Aiming deliberately at examination results, moreover, is apt to focus attention upon achieving the acceptable rather than upon what may be much more important: how the results are achieved.

In recent years there have been several movements in secondary schools both in Britain and the United States which have some promise for the future. There is certainly a new concern for 'process'—that is for the whole activity going on within the school and not just the measurable changes which exposure to a particular curriculum may aim to bring about. There is more dialogue between teachers and taught, even if instruction rather than a partnership in learning is what is offered. Even in O.E.C.D. circles 'educational planning' is less purely attentive to economic factors than it was. While it is becoming more concerned with educational issues proper, including indeed character building as well as subject content, it remains still much more interested in the education of the conscious part of the mind (e.g. 'decision making', 'moral education'), than the less conscious (attitude formation; the development of values and value-judgement).

Some of the most far-reaching experiments in Britain in re-forming the content of the curriculum at the secondary stage are those first encouraged by the Nuffield Foundation and then developed in new directions by the Schools Council. The Nuffield concern was to approach chemistry, mathematics, physics and biology in ways that revealed to the student at an early stage what the subject was really about. Some of the Schools Council effort has been directed to finding how an 'open' approach to these and other subjects could enable each to contribute to general education more effectively while not being robbed of its value as a special discipline with its own rigour. In particular the work in its 'General Studies 16-18' project seems significant and promising. One of the suggestions made by Robert Irvine Smith, who was in charge of it, is that boards for G.C.E. A-level examinations, used for university entrance purposes, should set compulsory 'open' papers or sections of papers designed for A-level economists, chemists, historians, etc., in which they are allowed to show how effectively they can think around a problem which is in their field but which can also be approached from other directions. As he points out, there is certainly no shortage of topics which raise moral, aesthetic, economic, political, sociological, biological and other questions (e.g. quality of life versus economic growth); topics which demand interdisciplinary treatment. Their adequate consideration, whether at the secondary or the tertiary stage of education, demands feeling, insight and imagination too. Even now the least likely capacities to be recognised are these—and we excuse ourselves by not acknowledging that secondary or tertiary education has any real responsibility for their development.

Chapter 7

Media of Influence

To see, hear and touch things is important in childhood not only because to sense can yield accurate observation but because by sensing we feel and experience the world vividly for ourselves—and find meaning in it. To be able to find a meaning in things is at all stages one of the basic necessities for education, and maybe for human development itself. It is a meagre concept of meaning which confines it to the solving of puzzles or problems that can be fully articulated: a great deal of learning in adolescence, and maturity too, is much less conscious than this. It is mediated by people who speak to us, maybe lecture to us, whose words we can read in books but with an increasingly subtle capacity to read the tone and the nuances as well as the surface meaning.

The subject matter studied will often be central in what we shall learn: there can indeed be no learning without subject matter. But how it is learned, the enthusiasm or coldness of the teacher, his fairness or his prejudices, obvious or concealed, will affect the meaning of what he teaches. The environment of a university or college can also have a powerful influence in extending or diminishing that experiential power in its students which remains important to the education they get from it. By environment I do not mean simply the physical environment—rather the mental climate of the department or honours school or residence hall or college. Those who contribute to a tradition of friendliness or austerity or competitiveness may include people long since dead. Standards of taste, acumen, judgement can be made manifest even in the form of the questions set for essays or the design of experiments to be done in a laboratory. Most students remain reachable through many channels down which a university's influence, if that university is alive, can flow. If some of these are impersonal and intellectual channels—argument, for instance, and the conveyance of undeniable fact—others bring more values into the picture than objective truth only.

An implicit culture indeed is latent even within the *idea* that lectures should be given, or experiments conducted by students themselves. It is latent too within university ceremonies and the long history upon which they draw; in the notion of a quadrangle, a campus, a Great Hall. Influence is conveyed through the genuineness with which a seminar is conducted. Priorities and omissions and silence in a discourse are themselves teachers, without anyone's necessarily being aware of the fact. Patterns of value are also mediated by the place a university gives to music making, travel, worship, political discussion, by the richness of experience it allows for. Patterns of value are inherent in its being a place where women and coloured people have equal (or unequal) rights with men and white people, by the permissiveness it offers its senior as well as its more junior members within limits which may be much more like those of a family than those of a school. Any such pattern can be disrupted or destroyed, but to the extent that its members fit in with it they are being influenced by it too. Even a reaction against it can show its influence. Here is *power*. It is, says Lionel Trilling (1966) perceptively, a person's culture which 'brings him into being in every respect except the physical, gives him his . . . habits of thought, his range of feeling, his idiom and tones of speech' (p. xii). The mental climate of a place of higher education will permeate minds that are permeable, and even modify their 'experienceability' itself to some extent.

Past and Present

A hundred and fifty years ago universities and colleges were more obviously communities than they are now. For one thing they were so much smaller. In most of the élite universities, moreover, the proportion of seniors to juniors was higher than it is today, and still higher than the economies of the 1970s and 1980s will make it. This was so in Cambridge and Louvain and Durham for example; Harvard and Princeton, Columbia and Swarthmore too. A hundred and fifty years ago there was a greater affinity of social class between teachers and taught; most of the tutors in English and American colleges 'lived in' and many were still unmarried. The universities and their colleges were more intimate in their atmosphere. But there was in society outside a dominant moral consensus which echoed that within the university itself to a greater degree than is any longer the case. An appreciable proportion of students too were studying under their tutors subjects which encouraged a transfer of values from tutor to student more conspicuously and openly than now: classical literature; philosophy in a pre-positivist era; mathematics, with its sense of order and certainty; law with its sense of tradition and authority; English or European or American history. The technologies were in these places studied by few, and even the sciences were largely studied in laboratories situated well and safely outside any of the colleges themselves.

The product of Oxbridge or the Ivy League universities of whom they were once most proud was essentially the gentleman amateur. A number of remnants of what was in many ways an aristocratic tradition were still to be discerned in the Oxford and Cambridge of the mid-twentieth century; some still are. The grey flannels and relaxed speech of the Oxford student until quite recent times, his delight in being unprophesiable, his anxiety to conceal his swotting, were among the trademarks. The Norfolk jacket of Edwardian days had given place to the sports coat, but the careful quest for a careless elegance remained. The tutor prided himself on writing his letters by hand, and the distinguished fellow of a college, if he was an arts man, preferred not to consult his MS. (or even have one) when he gave a lecture in public. For spontaneity and first-handness were virtues greatly prized. And the clublike spirit of the older Oxford and Cambridge, Trinity College, Dublin, Heidelberg and Marburg, and Cornell and Yale, has even yet, for those within the walls, not entirely been lost. These are all channels of influence.

It is not of course easy to separate out those influences which membership of a university community may bring to bear by reason of its being a university from those it communicates because it represents a particular and privileged sector of society. What is certain is that all universities have become to a lesser extent places of privilege. The social temper has become more democratic. The emphasis has shifted to subjects not involving so obvious a transfer of value judgements as did the classics, logic, law or history as they used to be taught.

Oxford and Cambridge today are places with some 11 000 students apiece as compared with 1 500 a hundred years ago—some of their colleges then being tiny indeed—and only some 4 000 even fifty years ago. The pure and the social sciences, the technologies, the humanities, often themselves dominated by a somewhat detached and scientific approach, are now the staples of study. And the assumption made in that approach is a powerful agent for shaping the kind of future we shall have. Universities can filter out many possible futures by their concepts of what is knowledge, the lead they give as initiators of research enterprises, the biases in approaching the world which they impart. They tend to underestimate the continuing importance of the senses and the feelings. If they separate the man or woman too completely from his own early past, they can prevent him from ever finding more than a superficial, intellectual, meaning in things. He may become an intellectual, innocent and proud, and be prevented by that from ever becoming experienced.

The élite universities, however, are no longer divided from other institutions of tertiary education in the way they were.

The proportion in them of the total number of students having tertiary education goes down annually and in most countries it will decline much further; and, significantly, they are no longer separated from the diversities and pluralities of outside society as much as they used to be. They belong to a computerised, urban world, with the telephone, radio and television able to penetrate everyone's living room.

Contemporary polytechnics and universities—including the most ancient—have much to learn from the past, whether their own past or that of other members of the family. But they have more, not fewer, functions to fulfil than used to be the case when the world was less de-humanising, and for a student population drawn from a much wider social range. Nor can they escape from any of their responsibilities by a simple failure to notice that they are mediators of influence or to take their educational job seriously—and that means more and more consciously than there was once any need for them to do. Many of their activities are still carried on even in the 1970s with a remarkable degree of unconsciousness. They involve unexamined premises that the scientists busy working inside them would certainly find reprehensible in their own procedures. Universities need to be in much more rigorous control of the means at their disposal for educating their students, and to tot up what their resources are. It is no longer enough that they should give their students the disciplines they will need as professionals. What is required is a receptive awareness of educational objectives, both social and personal, which is still quite rare among university teachers, who are anxious to toe the lines their continued professional reputation daily requires of them as chemists, historians, psychologists, but are by no means as conscious that the university or polytechnic of whose staff they are members is also a place of education whose demands may at times conflict with those of their professional guild.

What, then, are some of the specific means at our disposal, other than the content of the subjects we teach, for developing in students sensibilities, attitudes, human perceptions, as well as facts and skills? They still include a sense of belonging to the university itself (and this can have real influence even if it is an Open University); in many cases, residence in a new environment away from home whether in halls, flats or lodgings; the provision of special amenities for reading, looking and listening; the encouragement of particular kinds of contact with the world of work; and the way in which we teach our subjects. All offer opportunities for that broadening and disciplining of experience, that exercising of the affections and that challenge to reflectiveness about the human situation itself to which we have attached such importance.

Belonging to a University

Whether a student lives at home, in lodgings or a rooming house, in a flat or an apartment, in college or a hall of residence, he is going to be affected by his membership of a university community. Such socialisation may and probably will occur imperceptibly: he will be largely unaware of how he is being changed. But he *expects* to change: many students are disappointed in their university, especially in their first year when they are most open to be changed, because it seems too little interested in their development and too narrowly interested in life. Martin Trow may well be right in thinking that institutions with the most influence on students are those with a sense of their own uniqueness. Any university, however, inevitably stands for a number of values not so conspicuously emphasised outside it: a student's sharing of experiences with others who are intelligent and capable in a more than average degree of being literate or numerate will make him to some extent feel—at first perhaps uncomfortably—that he too now stands over against some of his more average or conventional contemporaries. This is more or less true even of students who take a radical line and appear to be in rebellion against their university or college. They are often in deeper rebellion against the conventions of society outside. Their wish for freedom to own and express ideas puts a strong emphasis on values which the university already rates more highly than society generally. Their desire for more participation in policy-making and syllabus-choosing activities of their college shows their wish to become more, not less, identified with some of its long-term purposes. If they hope that relations with men and women outside will become closer and do not want to be separated from them, they do not really want this to be at the expense of unorthodoxies, which show themselves not only in dress, but more significantly in ideas, ability to speak with fluency, lucidity and logic, unusualnesses which may very possibly in fact alienate them from the typical young worker.

In future a lower proportion of students is likely to come from the eighteen to twenty two age group. Instead, more will be mature students, who want to develop new interests or be re-educated for a career going off in a fresh direction. But it is quite wrong to think that these too will not need to belong to a university as a community and be influenced by such belonging. Birkbeck College, originally established in 1823 as the London Mechanics' Institute, but since 1920 a college of the University of London, has for generations been an outstandingly spirited place and a home to its students—though most of them have been part-time and during the whole of their degree course engaged elsewhere in London in full-time occupations. The Open University in Britain has from the start sought to personalise its teaching and to make as many as possible of its students into university students proper. It is quite unlike a body which awards merely external degrees. Its members of staff have been chosen not only for their scholarship but because they were interested in the *concept* of an Open University and anxious to teach in it. The hope was that their courses, whether on T.V. or mediated more sustainedly through books, packaged material and the kind of questions set, would involve both them and their students in a common enterprise. Its 237 Study Centres scattered throughout Britain, at which its students can meet in common rooms as well as use library and, in some cases, computer facilities, are a contribution to the spirit of the whole. So, much more, are the tutorial services which are based upon some 120 of the Study Centres, by means of which a counsellor can see each student on an average once a fortnight. Each of the two foundation courses in which a student enrols has a Summer School which the student is normally required to go to. And though each Summer School only lasts a week, attendance at it does help to build up in a student a sense that he belongs to a university—and to a continuing one.[1]

The Impact of Residence

It is significant that where a university has by tradition been collegiate and residential in the Oxford or Cambridge manner, the physical pattern of such residence has been of quadrangles surrounded by buildings so that the college was a kind of enclosure. The typical undergraduate was tutored, whether by himself or in company with another, in the tutor's own room, usually in his own College; he dined in the College on five or so nights a week and often lunched there, usually in the relative intimacy of the college hall, which significantly was not called a dining room, a restaurant or a cafeteria. It was the Oxford and Cambridge tradition of residence that gave most of the impetus in Britain and in Commonwealth countries to the movement towards halls of residence in modern universities whose wardens are academics and not, as in the United States, imported for the purpose.

A good deal of research has been done in recent years into the effects of residence in changing the outlook of students. Some of this has not been sociologically or psychologically subtle enough to yield results that are significant. Some has been too confined to a single university; some has relied overmuch upon students' and tutors' own estimates of the development that has taken place. But it is clear that students can be very differently affected by the experience of residence—it is probably not a matter only of particular kinds of temperament or particular atmospheres of individual halls, but a matter of

1 Cf. *The Early Development of the Open University.*

fitting the right temperaments to the right halls if maximum benefits are to be obtained. The 'press' of an institution can be powerful upon students who are impressionable along certain strata or in particular ways. It may be that what could be done easily by the experience of residence earlier in the century is not to be accomplished so easily now.

All the same there was a marked movement in Britain during the period 1945-65 towards the building of more residences for students. With notable exceptions, the chief motive was the need to provide roofs over heads, and to do it rapidly, for some proportion of the vast increase in numbers of students coming into higher education. Most of the new halls in British universities were built with help from national funds; in other countries where residence halls were put up in these years much more use was made of loan assistance from public or private sources. Some halls in Norway and Denmark, indeed, were established *ab initio* by student cooperatives and have been let in the three summer months ever since their foundation to tourists as hotel accommodation.

In the United States particularly, but in Britain too, there is astonishingly little evidence that in those years most of the student housing was conceived by anybody as having much educational importance. Riker's *Planning Functional College Housing* (1956), in spite of its clumsy and unpromising title, is one of the few American publications of the 1950s to show real awareness that dormitories could serve an educational purpose. Knox College, Illinois, was unusual in instructing the architects employed on building its new residences in the 1950s that they should be designed so as to encourage both study and socialisation in small groups. Far too many of the halls put up in the United States and in Europe for students were either much the same sort of thing which might have been erected as a luxury hotel on the one hand (with large lounges on the ground floor) or as a cheap hostel on the other. Privacy, quietness, encouragement to students to get to know one another as individuals, rooms for reading or browsing—or sound-proofed for music practice or listening to music—were rarely provided. Dining halls tended to be noisy. Even as late as the middle 60s in a number of countries the design of halls of residence was largely left to architects themselves, with little awareness shown either by academics or administrators that the style and spirit of a place where many students slept and ate and talked and worked could matter to their educational receptivity.

Since 1966 the rate of expansion of residential provision has slowed, partly because of financial difficulties but partly for other reasons. In the 1970s students are less and less willing to be circumscribed in the amount of freedom they are allowed; with votes at eighteen, a background of home life throughout childhood which has encouraged liberty, independence and pleasing oneself, and influences coming in from many directions during adolescence which emphasise wants and de-emphasise rules, it is not surprising that this should be so. The temper of the time involves, to use sociological language, a move away from shared value-systems 'towards a functional integration based on specialised roles which are mutually interdependent but which give rise to considerable personal autonomy, an emphasis on individual differences and flexibility in the regulation of relationships' (Bernstein, 1967). Even with the blossoming of the idea of the coeducational hall (with the University of Aberdeen surprisingly the first in Britain to introduce one when it opened its Crombie Hall in 1960), today students at many universities after their first year prefer to live in flats or apartments, if these are obtainable, whether in groups of four or six, or in pairs, or on their own. They argue that this is often cheaper, they are free to come in and out at any hour, to have meals at any hour, to invite their friends in at any time, go off unimpeded at weekends. And if this is an escape from 'educative influences' who minds? To be a member of 'a cohesive sub-community' not of his own choosing is not what a student today may be seeking anyway. In 1971-72 and 1972-73 in the U.S., many rooms in residence halls built in the 1950s and 1960s, both on older and newer campuses, could not be let at all. Students preferred to live in accommodation they had found for themselves, sometimes in downtown areas, often squalid, not unusually at a considerable distance from the campus. And there is a corresponding movement in Britain, though it has not gone nearly as far. With only a limited number of flats on the market, and those often expensive to rent, the demand for places in halls still remains enough to fill many more than all that are available. Few new halls, however, are now being built even in Britain, either with the aid of grants or loans from public or private money.

The pressure from government quarters is to have more students living at home. This, it is argued, will save money that needs to be saved and will not interfere with anything essential in the educational process. Much here may depend upon what is regarded as essential. Chickering (1969) has found evidence for believing that students who leave home to go to college or university are more consistent and rapid in their personal development than those who stay at home—though it seems to make little difference whether they live in hall or in lodgings.

Ought then the policy to be gradually to abandon the concept of the residential college? The most detailed sociological inquiry into residence in higher education known to me which has been done in Britain—and perhaps as yet in the United States—is reported by Joan Brothers and Stephen Hatch (1971). This is guarded in its answer to all policy questions. The authors say towards the end of their study:

'a broader experience is given in higher education by the complex mixture of institutional atmosphere, time for informal exchanges, staff encouragement of student mixing, a student culture that values such exchanges, and a common agreement that such mixing is valuable. Given all these elements, the provision of residential facilities for students can facilitate this exchange and give rise to the sense of common purpose and identity that are crucial to a community. But residence is likely to facilitate this exchange only when it is consciously used as an instrument to achieve such purposes. We have given instances where residence appears to be used successfully to achieve these aims. But there are also instances, historically and at the present time, where residence has been used institutionally to limit in various ways the personal development of young people; in which it has restricted their growth as mature and responsible citizens; where it has led to narrow and superficial communities that have not enlarged but have circumscribed their vision.

'In other words, residence is a tool of higher education. It is a particularly useful tool for humanising and personalising the system; for making large institutions feel small enough for the individual to be able to feel identified with them and capable of participating; and for widening the scope of higher education. It may indeed be the case that it is the *most* useful instrument for these purposes. But it must be emphasised that while residence has been used over a long period of time in this way, to reinforce and mediate the institution's basic goals, other possible tools have not really been fully tried' (p. 362).

It may be that halls in coming years should be chiefly places in which freshmen live, with a sprinkling of seniors. It may also be a good thing to try mixing students in some halls from several types of institution of higher education. It is certainly significant that many universities have found it difficult for thirty years now to discover enough members of the academic staff to take responsibility for colleges or halls. Half a generation ago, the Report of the U.G.C. Sub-Committee on Halls of Residence (1957) implied that a university might well not be able to go on having halls that mattered unless their wardens were given a quite new status in them. And they have not been given a new status. Too little time is given in most universities to considering, as questions of policy, media of influence on students, apart from the courses and curricula provided. An illuminating piece of research by Becker, Geer and Hughes (1968) in the United States which compared faculty and student views of the university experience shows clearly that the staff's concern—often exclusively—was the achievement of academic goals, whereas the students wanted their time in college and in hall to be much wider in its concerns.

Home and hall are both in any case sheltered environments compared with flats or lodgings. There is evidence that many students who move into lodgings or apartments after a year of residence in a hall choose to live with or not far away from friends they have made in hall. Being in lodgings can bring much stress, and loneliness too. Whether it does so for a larger or smaller proportion of students may often depend upon the temper of the university and the particular departments in it. Little research that is dependable has yet been done upon the effect of the spirit of a college or honours school on the lives outside college of its students. What is clear is that student discussions late into the night on a wide variety of personal, social and moral issues can be common in urban flats and lodgings far from college, and that students of both sexes from several institutions, and others who are not students, join in.[1] Such exchanges are still apt, however, to be affected greatly by some of the things learned in the university itself, not only information-wise, but attitude-wise.

It may well be that within ten or twenty years major changes in habit may occur that will make it easier for different uses to be made of halls and colleges and of university campuses themselves, from those that are at present common. The sharing of halls between institutions of diverse character advocated above as an experiment might help to solve some social, even some political, problems within a higher education system; it may be possible to fashion colleges with a corporate spirit which also offer more of the freedoms which students want, including contact with the outside world. With the coming upon the scene too of many more mature students, there may be radical changes of atmosphere on many campuses.

1 Source: J. Scherer, in Brothers and Hatch: *Residence and Student Life*, pp. 237–64.

It may be that the designing of universities in the future will be approached differently, with a community sense fostered by a greater variety of means. Some adumbration of this is the idea of structuring a university so that it forms 'an integrated pedestrian campus' (Perkin, 1969, pp. 90ff.) It will be designed, that is, or re-designed as opportunity occurs, in a form which, though it may be penetrated by people living in the area, makes it something like a large village in itself, having unity and intimacy. The campuses of Essex, Warwick, Lancaster, York and Bath Universities are notable examples; but the Bloomsbury and Kensington precincts of the University of London and the Chamberlin and Powell plan for Leeds, now at an advanced stage in its implementation, embody the same idea.

Opportunities for Personal Contacts

For many students, an increasing number perhaps, their most constant and intense associations will be with their fellows, senior as well as contemporary, in the department where they carry on their main studies. Some of these contacts will be made in lecture rooms, laboratories—and corridors—of the department itself. Laboratories are particularly good places for informal, as well as directed, conversation both between tutors, demonstrators and students and among students themselves. The test of right attitude for many a lecturer is whether he finds his students' viewpoints really interesting or worth listening to. By no means all meet the test! But there is a corresponding one to be passed by students in their attitudes to the viewpoints of their lecturers. Other contacts, essentially with the department as central focus, may occur both on or off campus in meetings of societies to which many members, senior and junior, of the department go, and in *ad hoc* groups which may meet anywhere, but nowhere more probably than over lunch in the refectory. There is plenty of evidence that students from the same department tend to sit in small groups together. Their talk will certainly not be confined to academic matters. The more the tradition of 9 to 5 'attendance' on the campus can be broken down the greater the opportunities for such discussions.

Some students (though in many universities quite a small percentage) take part in activities—political, religious and humanist, musical, dramatic, social—spread right across departmental barriers. Campaigns on topical issues may affect the outlook and ideas of many who never actually join in them, lectures by visiting 'firemen' may be listened to by hundreds, especially if they can be heard on closed circuit T.V. as well as attended in person, and student newspapers of a quality varying even from term to term have their influence. An intelligent editor has a job with more potentiality than he— or other people—normally realises. In these and other ways some contacts are or can be made within the campus between minds without regard to particular subject or professional interests.

But such broadening of interest and concern can be fostered off the campus too. Conferences which bring together students and members of staff from several, or many, universities— even across national boundaries—for the discussion of current issues are becoming more frequent. And in Europe the advent of the E.E.C. should make them more frequent still. Student travel is highly organised and may be hardly less significant in stretching and giving reality to ideas than the practice by which undergraduates spend a period during their degree course on some campus overseas. A sizcable number of American universities have offshoots in Europe at which students and faculty together may spend one or two semesters. Such an environment can be at once challenging to mind, more productive of contacts between specialists in different discip- lines than conditions at home allow, and of new understandings between students and their teachers. Those who have par- ticipated sometimes return to the main campus with a whole new concept of what university life means and of the degree of personal communication possible within it. In a slowly increasing number of cases today English undergraduates spend a period in another country as part of their course, learning to speak its language, to study its archaeology, geography or geology at first hand or to be associated for practical work with one of its industrial firms. All sorts of reasons can be found. The European Renaissance course in the History School at Warwick University includes one term, the first of the final year, in Venice to study some of the consequences of the Renaissance at first hand. It is significant that such arrangements, though catering sometimes for members of one department only, often succeed to a surprising extent in enlarging not only their knowledge of their subject but their awareness of other people as human beings.

Universities could without great financial outlay do much more than they do to help their students in their relationships with others. Encouragement to stay on the campus itself for longer hours can do something. Universities might well develop student houses of which home or non-resident students would be members on an inter-departmental basis, where there would be day-studies, reading rooms, common rooms, perhaps two or three bedrooms with beds available at a cheap rate, though on a one-nightly basis, for students who for special reasons were staying late at meetings in town or on the campus. Twenty years ago the University of Rochester in New York State equipped four rooms in its Women Students' Centre with six bunks each and let them to home students at 35 cents a night. They were much used by young women whose homes were unencouraging in their attitude to study. There has been great expansion in recent years in the provision of smallish cubicles with bookshelves and cupboard space for use as their own 'day-studies' by non-resident students in English colleges of education. The existence of such amenities can do much to keep students in closer contact with their college and to help it mean more to them.

In recent years in the United States a good deal of work has been done upon the effects of the 'climate' and temper of colleges and universities on student attitude. This is research very different from that concerned with institutional planning; its focal interest is people and their development and it is student-centred. It can lead to as many destructions of hypotheses as any other kind of research. High quality researches in this area are represented in P. E. Jacob's *Changing Values in College* (1957), Newcomb and Wilson's *College Peer Groups* (1966) and Feldman and Newcomb's *The Impact of College on Students* (1969).

It is clear enough from such investigations that sheer size in a university brings its own special brands of danger. If a community spirit is to be retained in a university of 8 000, 12 000, 25 000 or more students a far greater and a far more conscious effort has to be made to establish and maintain lines of communication than in a college of 2 000. The deep student malaise to which we referred in Chapter 4 is aggravated by the de-humanising effects of large, impersonal campuses. Whereas universities of between 8 000 and 30 000 students were uncommon until 1945 or even 1960 they are now acceptable in many countries, for example, in Japan, Britain, Scandinavia, Holland, Australia and in States of the U.S.A. where up to 1940 few institutions of higher education exceeded 3 000 students.[1] 'The more students there are', says Nevitt Sanford (1967), 'the more disconnected they tend to be from each other, from the faculty and from the administration. Attending larger classes, a student has less opportunity to know his teachers; and dealing with a largely impersonal bureaucracy, he is taught to regard himself less as a person than as a set of responses to institutional requirements' (p. 176). There is no answer to this except the finding of ways by which students come to know each other, and some of their seniors, as human beings as well as competitors, experts or scholars.

1 E.g.   Total student population:

	1938	1972
University of Amsterdam	2 438	14 000
University of Leeds	1 709	9 662
University of Sheffield	767	6 248
Michigan State University	5 623	39 542
University of California (Los Angeles)	7 911	29 661

The general ordering of the institution can make this easier or more difficult. If the first two activities a college lays on for its students are orientation and registration, with hours of standing in queues, it handicaps itself from the start in its ability to relate to them personally. If its tutors are concerned only with a student's examination prospects or the accuracy of the data he has amassed, that he shall follow the rules of the institution and the syllabuses of the course, the social pattern of relationships is bound to remain pretty formal, however courteous and pleasant the encounter and however frequent the chances of consultation. There will be no revelation of the tutor's own philosophy nor many discussions of things off beam. But a deliberate, too conscious, informality is at least as off-putting. Students in the 1970s may resent almost all provisions which appear to threaten their independence or adulthood, but a great many still warm quickly when a senior shows a real concern for them as people or, without patronage, takes a personal interest in their point of view. It is his availability which counts—not only in the sense that he can be relied upon to be physically *there* but that he is willing to give more of himself than anyone has a right to expect. He nourishes roots and gives freedom a chance to grow. The planning, architecture and physical amenities of a campus will certainly have influence. But the most permeating parts of our environment are its intellectual and moral standards, the interests and concerns of those whose rationality one respects: it is these that create the intimate environment in which the spirit can live.

No doubt more research is needed into how attitudes, resistances to suggestions, climates of hard work or non-work, are conveyed. But there is no substitute for personal relationships as media for some levels of education. I do not at all mean by this some sort of personal confession to individual students of what one believes in or doesn't believe in. That could be an infliction and could often have an element of self-boost about it, when what really matters is caring for other people—one's students in this case.

The lecture itself can sometimes be a medium for a personal relationship with listeners. The individuality of a lecturer's illustrations, his asides, his choice of words, make him more than a vehicle for fact or theory. If he outlines the arguments on two sides of a controversy or the case of two opposing theories he should not always conceal his personal view, even though making its status clear. A good deal more needs to be done by many professors and tutors to find out about their students simply as people. First names are of course much more often known (and used) than was once the case. But it can matter to know what town a student comes from, something about his leisure interests, the reading he is doing outside the subject, his ambitions. No one reading the personal type of reference still written by many Oxford and Cambridge tutors (though a diminishing proportion) about their students and comparing it with the corresponding statements—much more factual and impersonal—provided by tutors from other places could doubt that the Oxbridge people at least *think* they know their students better. It is certainly a personal kind of concern which is more likely to be powerful in its influence, whether for good or ill. One sometimes comes across a tutor who appears to be deeply interested in his students, who is warm and outgoing in manner, but who in fact has deceived himself (as well as sometimes his students) about the extent of his knowledge of them. Let him close his eyes; quietly substitute another student for the one he was talking to; and there may be little difference in the flow of talk. He may not even have noticed that a different student is now in front of him.

The student who emerges from his university with a good degree has not necessarily gained an education or an identity: that will depend as much as anything upon the disciplined knowledge, purposes and ideas he has gained through communication with other people there, both his contemporaries and his teachers. The more a college is a community encouraging both faculty and students to 'find' and to be themselves in it, the more powerful its influence.

The fact remains that it is difficult for most people to be

disciplined of mind or to have vision unless there are people around who are important to them. 'Inner controls', says Bruno Bettelheim (1961), 'are built up only on the basis of direct personal relations, not by obeying society's demands. They are only internalised when we identify ourselves with people we love, respect, or admire; people who have made these demands their own just as we did, by identifying with persons they respected . . . An age that offers so many chances for escaping personal identity because it offers so many comforts and distractions requires equal strengthening of the sense of identity' (pp. 96, 99).

Amenities for Reading, Looking, Listening

The library of most universities occupies physically a central place on the campus: that does not mean that its value as a liberalising agent or as a medium for informal general education is properly recognised. In many countries the salaries and status of even senior library staff compare unfavourably with those of academics and, in most, library grants fail dramatically to keep pace with the cost of books, and the grant makers are more and more reluctant to ensure that they do keep pace. In any economy drive it is easiest to cut library costs.

Few students in fact use a library purely and simply for consulting or borrowing 'set books'. This may be the only intention of some when they enter its doors. But given good servicing and apt disposal of its temptations a library can powerfully enlarge interests and stretch horizons: its periodicals room, its new accessions shelves, its reference section, can be effective media of general education. The concept of a library as a collection of books only is of course outdated. The next twenty years are likely to see a general acceptance of the idea that library services available to all students should include facilities not merely for duplicating and xeroxing but for looking at T.V. programmes live or recorded, for listening or re-listening to lectures on tape, for connecting users to data banks and computer programmes held elsewhere. There is much to be said for housing a bookshop and shop where tapes and cassettes can be bought either in or near the library.

Students' Unions today are far too often little larger than they were when the university had half its present numbers of students. In some universities and polytechnics they can be grossly overcrowded, squalid places. There are many opportunities that might be taken if there is space, money, and spirit; areas for example given over to exhibitions or photographs and paintings well and strikingly displayed; rooms for browsing, reading, typewriting, chess-playing; others for film making and showing, music, pop and classical, social dancing, meetings of clubs in great variety.

Contacts with the Outside World

Many of the contacts a university makes with the world are contacts on a subject basis with other scholars and research workers, not only within the home country, but many others. The whole spirit of a place can be altered by such out-goingness. So can perception of what it is really important to research into: many research projects not only for Ph.D. purposes but far beyond that stage are out of touch and a waste of time. One of the most obvious differences between universities and colleges of high rank and those which are more provincial is in the scope and range of their outside contacts. Contacts on a departmental basis with industry, schools or social work can be a great asset. Too often at present they are overcautious and lack flair. Universities would gain greatly from being in touch more often with the actualities of both industrial and political life. They need to be detached, it is true, but they also need to know more realistically what the problems are that have really to be thought about. We need a freer flow of people in both directions between the world outside and the universities.

One of the insufficiently recognised benefits of the 'sandwich' principle has been the closer relationships, personal as well as institutional, between colleges and industry which they have fostered at many levels. Relationships with schools, however, (and industry itself, too often) still tend to be self-interested and subject orientated: far less concerned with the quality of the general education the school may be giving its students than with its effectiveness in equipping those about to enter universities with expertise in subject fields; too much confined to the examinational attainments of its products. For a number of reasons the years sixteen to twenty make a unified period, as an increasing body of thoughtful opinion in England argues; the more the pity therefore that contacts between institutions of secondary and of tertiary education tend to be so tenuous, superficial and academically limited.

A university which is to be liberally educative needs to reduce chances of misunderstandings between itself and schools and between itself and industry; but to do this without sacrificing its own *raison d'être*, its sense of the importance of research or of accurate scholarship. Such an outgoingness will be clear to its students: it could increase the attractiveness of the education it gave them besides improving its quality.

Conclusion

In spite of what is being done the provision made by institutions of higher education for socialising their students or themselves is far from enough, and even what is done by the left hand is often done without the right hand knowing. All such provision may be seen as peripheral to the real work of the university, and barely related to it, which is still conceived as training students to know and to think within a given area. The knowledge and the thought are often, however, more superficial and more irrelevant than they should be because experiencing power has been left, uncultivated, to shrivel. Universities are by no means enough aware of what Sigmund Koch has called 'the mass dehumanisation process which characterises our time—the simplification of sensibility, the homogenisation of taste, the attenuation of the capacity for experience.' But the process continues apace. And admittedly, if we don't know what else we want to be, it may be a relief to follow the clear purpose of making ourselves—and other people—into organisation men, useful, it may be, at least as instruments in one way or another.

Chapter 8

The Content of the Curriculum

All institutions of higher education need, as we have been implying, to be communities, and communities in which both rigorous expression of thought and disciplined expression of feeling will find encouragement. For most students in these days it is their department that is likely to be the focus of their interest, and within that department the subject or subjects they are studying. However admirable the 'facilitating environment' a college or a campus may appear to provide for teaching or research, the real test will be whether sound teaching and research are in fact facilitated by it. Undoubtedly the environment in which they occur will affect the orientation and content both of research and education: a de-personalised, antiseptic mental climate will make it all but impossible to teach some things, but a do-as-you-please one may make it all but impossible to teach others.

The teaching given in a university is essentially of subjects—whether they are taught singly, or in multi-disciplinary combinations, or are more organically united into new interdisciplinary forms. Whether it is a single field or not, a subject must have a recognisable coherence and make demands upon the mind. Some well-known subjects cultivate a more definable territory than others—anatomy, pure mathematics and economics, for example. English literature, on the other hand, is a whole colony of subject areas and may demand a wide-ranging exercise of the modes of knowing from its students.

'Hard' scientific knowledge may be required; but other modes of apprehension will be needed too, including most of those listed by Paul Hirst (Dearden, Hirst and Peters, 1972) in his categorisation of the modes or ways of knowing: besides the empirical he includes the logical, the aesthetic, the historical, the moral and the religious (pp. 400-8).

What is called mental discipline is produced by an exercise of mind in studying at depth some aspects of a subject or the same aspect of a number of subjects. One subject may yield several disciplines. Though a course which is a single subject course can be wide in its range there are many temptations to encourage students at the tertiary stage of their education to concentrate narrowly. The narrowness may be caused by a vocational emphasis, or one that is research-orientated. There may be cut-throat competition for particular kinds of job facing the graduate when he gets out into the world. From this side of society there is the argument that experts are needed, serviceable experts who will direct their energies, at any rate in their working hours, down one avenue. Yet there is a widespread discontent at the inadequacy of the experts we produce, not merely because they seem uncivilised in their leisure hours but because of their blinkered sight and non-reflectiveness in working hours too. Some of the inadequacy is caused by their lack of *education*. They have not been introduced at depth to a wide enough range of subjects during their studies: they have not really seen basic connections between subject areas or come sufficiently to know things from different angles—exercising enough of the different ways of knowing.

Concern about the curriculum in higher education has been manifest for nearly two centuries now but it has grown rapidly in the last few years. The curricular element in the three-year course which eighteenth-century young gentlemen took in Oxford or Cambridge was not necessarily considerable at all. Indeed, until the emergence from 1800 onwards of a system of competitive examinations leading to honours degrees and in their turn to careers, there was little encouragement to undergraduates in England to study either in depth or with strenuousness. Scholarships and Fellowships were generally confined to founders' kin, to boys coming from named schools or who had been born in particular parts of the country. Their teachers were appointed from among the Fellows and one tutor often gave his students virtually all the teaching they would receive during their college course. The aim was rather to dye the student a certain colour than to make him into a scholar or an expert of any sort. The diet of studies for most was a classical one; there was, or it was thought that there was, a certain propriety in reading the classics and a relationship between doing that and acquiring manners and gentility. The power of Oxford and Cambridge in eighteenth-century England stemmed rather from their aristocratic, liberal climate than the mental exercise they gave to many of those who would run the country. With the need of the State for better trained ministers and civil servants, especially the latter, in a growing complex nineteenth-century world, Oxford, Cambridge and to some extent London all developed courses for specialised and classified honours degrees. The competition inherent in such a system was a reflection of competition in the business and political world outside.

One powerful influence in making the curriculum, and particularly specialisation within it, more central in English university education was the growth in importance of scientific research fostered by the German example—at first in pure rather than applied fields. Another powerful influence was the availability of external degrees in a wide variety of subjects offered by the University of London, where most of the weight had necessarily to be placed upon knowledge and its organisation within the mind. It became progressively more respectable for a large proportion of students to be specialists, though until late in the century and even beyond it the ambition of some of the cleverest men at Oxford and Cambridge was to take a double first or its equivalent in so disparate a combination as classics or classics/philosophy and mathematics. Here perhaps may be seen the concept of the widely educated university man having a last fling in its older form.

A curriculum decision which had to be made in British universities in the nineteenth century was whether applied science and, indeed, applied studies generally should come within the university orbit. This is a battle still going on in such fields as social work, home economics, even education. But much of it has been decided: in British universities engineering and the applications to industry of the chemical and physical sciences are familiar parts of the undergraduate and post-graduate curriculum. They are not relegated for study to special institutes—whether undergraduate or post-graduate or both—as in a number of continental countries and in Russia. And the example of, for instance, London and Liverpool, Leeds and Glasgow has to a considerable extent been followed by Oxford and Cambridge themselves. But the coming into being of first degrees in applied science made it seem more than ever natural for the content of undergraduate courses to be pre-professional. The utilitarianism of the nineteenth century both of middle-class Europe and the United States could rejoice in such a fulfilment. But the orientation towards research of many undergraduate honours courses in the pure sciences, and increasingly in arts subjects, was also in fact no less pre-professional—though with less justification, since only a small fraction of graduates would ever become professional research workers.

In Scotland there was a powerful tradition of ordinary degrees which until recent years compelled most students who would proceed to honours to take a range of subjects to pass standard first. But it must be admitted that in many cases these did not add up to a coherent whole in the student's mind. Nor can the adoption of the principle of 'electives' by American universities for the curriculum of first degrees, following the example of Cornell in the 1860s, be seen as a really adequate alternative to specialisation or professionalism. Under the elective system each student could choose within wider and wider limits between a large number of courses and in this way make up the content of his own degree course. In 1884 only seven out of sixteen freshmen courses at Harvard were compulsory and all the courses in the following three years were elective.[1]

A curriculum of subject specialisation, whether leading to a professional career or to a career in research, has appeared to stand obviously self-justified as useful and beneficial to society either in the near or in the further future. On the other hand, a curriculum so general and so student-centred as to consist of a fairly random choice of electives in practice has also appeared to be justified because the freedom of the student has seemed to be a sufficient cause. Both types in different ways are, however, the product of societies not very sure of their own goals.

Clear certainty about its goals is hardly to be obtained in a modern society, however desirable it may be so to educate undergraduates within it that they have insight and humanity, and are concerned both subjectively and objectively with issues of social purpose. Any curriculum for a first degree which will be educative in such ways must depend, if it is to attract more than a very few students, upon the prospect it opens up of a career that will be interesting and will bring with it a good income, good social status or both. If this was largely true at periods when society had far more coherent aims and beliefs than now, it is even more the case today. Courses for first degrees must not be 'general' or 'interdisciplinary' at the cost of shedding their students. Meaning must have people to realise it!

The years between 1920 and 1940 in the United States saw several powerful but fruitless efforts to build up a demand that students should receive a basic general education before going on to graduate work. These were perhaps more the product of a few provocative and enthusiastic advocates than a widely based movement. Alexander Meiklejohn at Annapolis and Robert Hutchins at Chicago were prophets who converted or compelled a following; but they needed a more propitious climate for the trees to grow tall whose seeds they sowed. That climate is still not with us. Nor is it likely that a diet of

1 Source: James, Henry: *Charles W. Elliot, President of Harvard University 1869/1909*, New York, 1930, p. 260.

fifty or a hundred of the 'best books' studied at depth is the right one even for intelligent students whose motivations to take degree courses are not particularly academic. But the vision and imaginative planning ahead which led in Britain to the issue of the McNair Report and the design of a great Education Act in 1944, led in the United States after the war to the new and practical thinking behind the Harvard Report of 1946 on *General Education in a Free Society*. And within Harvard in particular for a number of years it had its influence.

Predominantly, however, the two great wars of this century acted as further encouragement to places of higher education to produce people qualified in scientific and technical ways. As we saw earlier, many people in Britain in 1940 thought that the universities would be depopulated if the war continued for any appreciable time. Instead they became training grounds for the greater and greater numbers of experts and specialists the nation required. Such directed demands have continued, among the causes being the pursuit of affluence by the developed countries and the calculating rationalism dominant in both capitalist and communist countries. It was the number and complexity of the analytical skills required which rapidly enlarged the demand for higher education. A channelling of mental energy down narrow avenues can yield dividends—with trained and clever economists, computer scientists, engineers, surgeons, research chemists, management experts, in great demand these last thirty years. On both sides of the Atlantic, however, the 1950s were years in which idealism in universities, including a concern with general education, was subjugated to what seemed an overriding need for the production of specialists and professionals—a view which still predominates in spite of the significant efforts to replace or modify it.

The enthusiasm with which the Harvard Report on *General Education* mentioned above was followed up has lessened greatly. Both the terms 'liberal' and 'general' education have lost repute in the postwar years—partly because of the mushiness associated with such phraseology, partly because 'liberal education' has an aristocratic flavour about it, a soupçon of untemptable éliteness, which is now heartily disliked. In a modern democracy the phrase coined by the Carnegie Commission to replace it—'a broad learning experience'—may conceivably avoid these dangers. Such experience, however, must usually be given the student in the context of a vocation he comes to see as worthwhile; and if it is to be adequate in scope and depth it must involve feeling, sensibility and imagination as well as thought.

These provisos are both likely to rule out any possibility of a complete unloading upon Liberal Studies Departments of the older type in institutions of higher education of the task of giving students what is required. However devoted their lecturers and however concerned their lectures and seminars, it is clear enough from the reactions of many, though by no means all, of their students that the recipe has so far been but tepidly successful. Liberal Studies are apt to be regarded by most students as minor activities, an extra to which it is not necessary to bring one's shrewdest concentration. The real attitude of some colleges—backed by public opinion—to such departments may perhaps be shown by their time-tabling of student's work so that they devote two or three hours a week to Liberal Studies in their first year or two years and then no more. In other places, including some technological universities and polytechnics, the Liberal Studies offerings may be spread much more generally through the course, though they rarely occupy more than twelve per cent or so of a student's time or comprise more than one or two units of work a week. It is hoped no doubt that, somehow, the T.V. programmes which they will go on watching in their leisure, or the periodicals they see, or their unprogrammed discussions with friends, will suffice to continue their non-specialist education. Today students are not likely to achieve this in sufficient measure unless they have first been motivated to look for a more profound relevance in what they watch, hear and read than is compatible with the casualness of the demand made on them. The extent of the selectivity a student needs to exercise presupposes a degree of commitment of which he may never have supposed himself capable—except, it may be, within the territory of his specialism itself, and there with his intellect used as an instrument rather than with an undivided mind and heart.

It cannot be denied, however, that the obstacles to giving most students a liberalising tertiary education today are formidable. There is little time in which to do it. The lines laid down by professional guilds and by modern life itself for universities and polytechnics to toe are exacting. The sheer amount of knowledge and skills to be attained by the student if he is to be licensed as a doctor, an engineer, a psychologist, a psychiatrist, a lawyer, are great and there is no substitute for them. But the undisturbed contentment of many specialists with a specialist approach to their subject has also been an obstacle. Many university teachers—though potentially excellent at teaching—have not been interested enough in teaching or motivated strongly enough to be concerned even to teach well what they know so well. Nor have they seriously considered the kind of *person* they would most like to produce as a result of the teaching. It may not have appeared to them as their function to give really personal education through their subject itself, whether or not they were interested in students outside the lecture room or laboratory. Had they been able to believe that this was part of their job they might have been horrified at the chances they failed to take and at the meagre sort of man or woman which was all their instruction catered for. The concept in the mind of its teachers of what properly belongs to a subject and what does not will have been largely determined by tradition. A number of specialist fields are, however, more capable than is often realised of being tilled so that they yield an education that is humane and wide without sacrifice to their central subject matter.

Though more resolute efforts have been made in recent years in many places of higher education to create degrees of high standard which combine several subjects in more or less flexible combinations, it has not proved easy to get these accepted as of equal worth with single subject specialisms. In many of the joint honours degrees in disparate pairs of subjects at civic universities some of the difficulty is caused by each subject being taught as itself a specialism, too little attention being paid to common elements. In joint honours schools, of which there is a rapidly increasing number, it is still in the 1970s not unusual for each head of a separate department—English and philosophy, Latin and music, chemistry and management, for example—to be more jealous of the standing of his 'own' subject than anxious to secure that the joint degree is really a living whole rather than a piecing together of parts. And graduates with a joint honours degree, a general degree with honours, or a degree that is interdisciplinary in character even today find it difficult to be accepted at a university—especially one other than their own—for higher degree purposes, especially to read for a research degree, in one of the fields they have studied. For they have had insufficient grounding in it and there may well be no research degrees involving the combination of subjects they have studied. The fact must be faced too that the introduction of satisfactory joint honours schools or of 'interdisciplinary' combinations of subjects demand an immense amount of work on the part of those who produce and will teach them—and not only hard work, but humility and willingness to see the other viewpoints as well as a clear sense of why the study of a single subject, or of two or more subjects separately, is not likely in future to be an adequate educational recipe for large numbers of students. For some—and among them some of the most intelligent—a three-year concentration virtually upon a single specialist subject may continue to be best.

One of the best surveys of what has so far been done in the United States to change the specialist approach to the content of first degrees is Dressel and DeLisle's *Undergraduate Curriculum Trends* (1969). They were not more than moderately impressed by what had been accomplished up to 1967. 'Despite all the talk about innovation', they say, 'undergraduate curricular requirements as a whole have changed remarkably little in the ten years (1957-67)' (p. 75). 'The significant area for innovation lies in re-thinking the total undergraduate program in an attempt to resore unity and relevance. The evidence on such activity is discouraging' (p. 76). All the same they show that at least there was pressure to break away from unprincipled collectivities of units and from specialisation seen as a satisfactory end in itself.

Contemporary catalogues both of American and Canadian universities contain many fine statements about the integrated nature of the courses offered, as this excerpt from one of them, which is typical of many others, shows: 'The curriculum leading to the B.A. Degree is designed to provide students with general and specialised studies in the liberal arts and to prepare students for postgraduate studies or for admission to other higher professional or occupational studies. The organisation of the curriculum, therefore, is designed to acquaint all beginning students with the wide range of contemporary knowledge in the various disciplines which compose the humanities, social sciences, and natural sciences. To this end, First Year students follow a common program, which is meant to provide them with an integrated and engaging exposure to important questions relating to man, his ideas and institutions, and his physical environment.' What one wonders is how far the integrating may have to be done simply by the student himself.

During the past few years one of the universities keenest upon mounting a programme of coherent and meaningful courses for undergraduates has been the Santa Cruz campus of the University of California. Each of its colleges was designed to give a different kind of liberal education to its students; the planning was imaginative, careful, scholarly. In addition to taking courses put on by the university each man or woman was and still is required to take part in a college programme: a sequence of courses, involving lectures and active membership of seminar groups. There is a wide choice and some highly attractive offerings, usually of an interdisciplinary sort, are available. At Cowell College the emphasis is on world civilisation; in Stevenson it centres on modern social thought; in Crown it is on the dependence of society upon scientific developments of very varied kinds.

Such carefully worked out and demanding courses in the colleges call for great devotion from members of staff, with much new reading and thinking, often in disciplines which are not the tutor's own. What if the staff are unwilling? There is a conflict in the minds of many of them between devotion on the one hand to their college and on the other to their specialist discipline. Concentration on a special area, they believe, is the only way to a change of post—and mobility is part of the American way of life for many—or promotion to a full professorship anywhere. And the intra-university test of the quality of a department is still the research it does rather than the quality of the education it provides. A young university in another part of the U.S., proud of its East Asian Studies Department, and asked in 1972 why that department was judged to be so good, replied, 'Look at how many of the papers it has produced have been read at conferences of real scholars!' Whether the department catered for the needs of the students who actually went to the university seemed not to be a point at issue. A dichotomy between devotion to what might appear the best interests of one's students and devotion to the advancement of a subject has of course its counterparts on British and European campuses. Publications of a scholarly sort are as it were investments by the scholar to establish his standing in a non-money economy—to give him the confidence which in a different social setting might be brought by an hereditary title or a comfortable affluence.

Though more resolute efforts have been made in recent years in a number of universities to secure degrees of a genuinely interdisciplinary sort, it is easy to over-estimate the extent of the change. An entirely free choice given to students to combine units together for degree purposes is obviously not going to yield enough coherence unless there is counselling of the highest quality and a remarkably cohesive staff. And such counselling is rare.

In some places, however, degree course patterns are becoming available which link studies meaningfully, the combinations of major and major or major and minor which are allowed being under an adequate measure of control. What is disappointing still is the infrequency with which a mixture of science subjects with arts subjects is permitted after the first year and the even greater infrequency with which it is encouraged. A robust change in course structure requires an equally robust change of attitude and of preconception on the part of the teachers concerned; and this is obviously difficult to produce, though the new B.Ed. degree in Britain has its promise. Efforts to produce a genuinely interdisciplinary curriculum throughout the whole of a first degree course are rare anywhere in Europe, though it must be remembered that in most European countries the later years of school life involve the study of a wide range of subjects—humanities, mathematics and sciences, even though in separation from each other—to an appreciably higher academic level than the entering freshmen even at a high quality university in the U.S. or Canada will have pursued. In England the majority of young people still at school between sixteen and eighteen have in the past fifty years been encouraged to concentrate most of their effort during those years upon three subjects, usually all sciences or all humanities, though recently in a noteworthy and now rapidly growing proportion of cases drawn from both groups.

In the last generation more people (though far from enough) in higher education in Britain have become aware of the importance of thinking anew about the relevance and the potential of the courses and disciplines they teach. In the years ahead powerful pressures will be making for change, of which the greatly increased numbers and increasingly varied motivations of students entering universities and colleges are two.

The physical and communication needs of a society rapidly increasing in its complexity call for further changes in the content of tertiary education—in other words for the curriculum development to which so much thought has been given in recent years at the secondary stage. Many of the problems of congested, city-dwelling populations, dependent more and more upon technology, can only be solved by intellectual team-work. The provision of concurrent and sandwich courses can have lively advantages. At the postgraduate level the spread of research centres which brings to bear the resources of separate disciplines upon the solution of common problems should result in due course in the creation of teachers who can take back to their undergraduate classes a new concept of the possibilities of new approaches to the teaching of particular subjects. Centres of Population Studies, Urban Studies, Area Studies, Communication Studies, for instance, could be significant in their impact. In every advanced country the proportion of people in the service industries is going up rapidly. The need grows for educated managers, administrators, social and welfare workers, teachers, transport planners, and many others whose expertise is non-isolationist. It is not only or even primarily a research orientation that they need; but they do require enough awareness of the nature and importance of research to be able to identify the inquiries that are most relevant and to be able to use with judgement the findings which come out of them.

A more profound influence is the change in society's ideals about its own direction of progress; it has on the one hand an urgent need for relevantly trained experts, but on the other a deeper need, more slowly rising to consciousness, for far more people who have arrived at personal, thought-out convictions about the worthwhile.

There are some signs that we may have begun now to move into a new period in curriculum construction in university degree courses, however pragmatic and counter to what is still majority opinion some of the moves have been. Admittedly the Oxford Greats school, which evolved during the nineteenth century, is itself a combined honours school of classics and philosophy—essentially, as Daniel Bell has pointed out (1966, p. 286), a training in a way to read texts so as to produce a mind of distinctive quality. But it is only of recent years that there have been in England attempts that were at all widespread to produce degree courses involving several subjects in a thought-out coherence. The movement has been increasing in scope, range and conscious control since 1945. It was in 1947 that general honours degrees, first in arts and then in science, began to be introduced in many universities. Other tide marks are provided by the Keele curriculum of 1949, the abolition of Faculties and the ingenious new structuring of degree courses at Sussex (1961), East Anglia (1964), Lancaster (1964), Ulster (1965), Aston (1966), Surrey (1966), and elsewhere; the introduction at Oxford of honours schools in engineering science and economics; in psychology, philosophy and physiology; and from 1970 in the human sciences; the adoption in numerous places, including most polytechnics and the Open University, of a modified unit system; and a widespread growth of one-year M.A. and M.Sc. degrees of a non-research type. Further signs of evolution are the tendency to give more freedom to students to choose options within a single honours subject to fit their shape of mind—for example, the imaginative new honours degree in English at University College, London; the greater flexibility allowed to students in many places to choose subjects with which to support their main specialisation; and some relaxing of special subject requirements for entry to honours schools.

Efforts to broaden the courses of study for arts degrees or science degrees in recent years in Britain can be divided into attempts to enlarge the coverage of subjects within a predominant specialisation either in science or arts, and attempts to include at some stage in a degree course a somewhat more interdisciplinary approach involving both arts and science.

It is widely recognised in Britain that the old type of pass degree made up of a miscellany of subjects taken in combinations often determined fortuitously (including as a factor the catching of the right bus home on, say, Tuesday and Thursday afternoons) is not the answer in an age of specialisation. It is realised in the United States that general education at the tertiary level is not going to be produced by those who submit themselves to it unwillingly, feeling it to be irrelevant. The best answer in practice, it is most often argued, must lie in a widening of the spread of subjects within the sciences or the arts themselves to give an equipment of knowledge and skills that is more adequate to the needs of the market and of modern society, a society in which men are far more aware than they were of the importance of ecological, psychological and sociological factors. It is more often the honours schools in applied science than those in arts or pure science which have given students an opportunity to extend their knowledge in this way. In recent years, however, two influences have caused a widening in the subject scope of some degrees which can be taken in faculties of pure science. One is the growth of research interests in territories in the borderland between chemistry and physics, physics and medicine, biology and chemistry. Biochemistry has for a long while now been a recognised first degree subject in many universities. Of more recent creation under the same general influence have been degree combinations involving more or less carefully worked out linkages between two disparate subjects, though often a degree of this type may involve four instead of three years. Chemistry-physiology; geography-geology; zoology-psychology are among numerous examples of such joint degrees which can be taken at many civic universities.

The other influence making for a larger scope in some first degree syllabuses in science has been a conscious demand from some students—small in total number but high in quality—for a curriculum which would enable them to consider seriously some of the problems raised by science and technology; their implications for the environment and human values. Among the pioneer degrees of this type is the B.Sc. in Liberal Studies in Science of Manchester University. There are departments or units in the science faculties of several large civic universities in Britain which seek to make students specialising in particular sciences more conscious of the history, philosophy and modern significance of their field. Notable and imaginative work, for example, is being done by the Science Studies Unit at Edinburgh and in the Integrated Science course at the University of Aston in Birmingham. In the first year of the Aston course the physical, biological and social sciences are taught as three distinct courses with some cross-reference between them. In the second and third years in the course on scientific method the methods used in the first year are abstracted and critically discussed, but the main concentration is on three topics: 'Materials', 'Systems' and 'Science, Technology and Society'. In the last of these some modern dilemmas arising out of the increased use of technology are examined in as much depth and detail as possible—e.g. the production of waste, pollution, possible exhaustion of natural resources, ecological problems, problems of financing desirable projects, criteria for innovation, etc. All this promises to do much to open up students' minds. In what proportion of cases it will sensitise them to more personal and individual human problems, or alert them to the dangers as well as the strengths of the technological frame of mind itself, awaits the event.

A good deal of thinking is going on about possible future shapes for courses in science which, while specialist, should be orientated to society as it is, that is should be more 'relevant'. Thus Professor Norman Greenwood of the Department of Inorganic and Structural Chemistry at Leeds was in line with a body of contemporary opinion when at the meeting of the British Association in September 1971 he advocated a new type of honours chemistry course. Chemistry, he argued, should be treated as a scientific discipline within the wider context of our present society. Less emphasis should be placed in this on manipulative skill in the laboratory, though practical work would still form a large and crucial component of the course. Lectures in his own courses are designed to indicate the implications and ramifications of the chemistry being studied, and tutorial work is supplemented by seminar discussion. Great emphasis is placed on extended preparation for intellectually testing essays; these, he believes, develop a facility for information research and for assessment and judgement which chemistry students taking more conventional courses often lack.

The prime begetter of the imaginative Keele curriculum experiments already referred to was Lord Lindsay, who for much of his life had been a tutor and lecturer in the Oxford Greats school and had himself helped to introduce at Oxford the course in Modern Greats, which was a mixture of studies in philosophy, economics and politics. The foundation courses at Keele represent a strenuous, pioneering attempt to give every student an introduction, lasting a whole year, to a wide range of knowledge, and so enable him to choose open-eyed what he later takes as his major and minor specialisms. All first year students at Keele must attend the general course which includes some 230 lectures distributed through the session, and consists of three elements: (i) the 'main thread' in which the general development of the earth and of human progress is traced from the emergence of life, through the ancient civilisations to the present day; (ii) a 'discursive treatment', with specific lectures on particular problems and developments bearing on the rights and duties of man; and (iii) periodic lectures on 'recurrent topics', including philosophical questions, the idea of nature, the creative arts, social change and religious belief. As well as discussion groups on the main lecture course, a student is also required to take two 'sessional' courses of weekly classes through the year on subjects he has not studied before (including science for non-science students, for example), together with three 'terminal' courses lasting one term each, normally on subjects he has studied at school and with which he will probably continue after the foundation year is over. To ensure breadth the sessionals and terminals must be distributed between all three Boards of Studies: humanities, social sciences and natural sciences. In this way the student is prepared for the remaining three principal years of his course, in which he must take two subjects at principal level, each for three years, and two at subsidiary level, each for one year. Of the four subjects, one must be chosen from the arts and social sciences and one from the natural sciences.[1]

That the continuing experiment has been to a considerable extent a success is shown by the favourable comment of a large proportion of ex-Keele students. There are some criticisms. Mountford (1972) quotes a former President of the Keele Union: 'At present Keele students spend their first year learning the inter-relatedness of human experience and knowledge; and spend their next three years in Departments which are jealously upholding the sanctity of disciplinary barriers. The Faculty at Keele have on the whole been less faithful to the idea of Keele than have many of the students' (p. 266). He goes on to say, however, that the evidence is strong that the foundation year taken as a whole has proved its effectiveness. 'The lecture course, though possibly too encyclopaedic, has been carefully thought out, is well balanced and is very well taught; apart from its relative failure to give non-science students a feeling for the methods of scientific thinking, it broadens the outlook of students and is regarded by graduates as a particularly valuable part of the curriculum' (p. 281).

The establishment and continuation of the Keele Foundation Year has encouraged specialists to look at their subjects from a new viewpoint and to try to make them palatable to non specialists. It has certainly brought many members of staff closer together both in planning and assessing their teaching jointly with others. But this is still some distance from deliberately or closely interrelating disciplines—or even ensuring that all the modes of knowing will be exercised during the year concerned. Nor in the courses at Keele which follow the first year do the specialists seem to make great attempts to use its width as a real foundation for their own syllabuses—which are, though for understandable reasons, very like those at other places.

Each of the group of universities founded in the early 60s

1 This summary draws upon the admirable account made by Perkin (1969), p. 118.

was encouraged in discreet and English ways—for example, by the careful composition of the planning committee, by the advice given it about the selection of its first Vice-Chancellor, by the choice of site and architect—to develop along its own lines. They were all intended to be primarily places for undergraduate study and most came to provide a one-year mastership course, not too research-oriented or over-specialist, to follow the bachelorship, as was indicated in Chapter 3. The struggle to retain such a concept against the tide has not been wholly successful. For the pressures to produce students fitted to go straight on to graduate work in a specialised field elsewhere have continued to be powerful, as has strong encouragement to the academically ambitious member of staff to produce works of scholarship in one particular field rather than several, or rather than works in interdisciplinary areas. The words 'smatter', 'superficial', always used in a derogatory sense, could be dropped lightly into the air as one talked about graduates from these newest universities or some of their teachers. The very concept of Schools of Study originated by Sussex and followed in one form or another by most of the others was not altogether approved in conventional circles. One natural defence was for the new universities to develop, with Foundation support, graduate work of their own in centres or units—as for example the Centre for Educational Technology at Sussex, that for Science Education at East Anglia, that for Higher Education at Lancaster. To take the initiative is often the best answer to criticism; attack, the most effective defence.

The most serious comments upon the theory of general education embodied in the curricula of this group of new universities have come not from works which were theoretical in their stance but in two books largely descriptive in intent: *The Idea of a University* about Sussex, with an outstanding chapter by Asa Briggs (1964) on redrawing the map of learning, and Perkin's *New Universities in the United Kingdom* (1969).

In the University of Sussex a student normally studies his

main subject within the work of a school—e.g. a School of European Studies or Social Studies or English and American Studies—in which he shares courses with students taking other subjects as their majors. He could gain a different orientation to his main subject if he studied in the context of one school rather than of another though he might attend the same lectures in, say, modern English history if he attended them within the School of Social Studies or the School of European Studies. In addition to the schools system there is an arts-science programme which very consciously crosses dividing lines. According to Goodlad (1973), however, the view is widely held that since the mid-60s the liberal temper at Sussex has become somewhat less encouraging to inter-school work and emphasises less the importance of bridging the arts-science divide (pp. 130-3).

Embedded in some of the most interesting interdisciplinary courses is the notion of relating areas of experience. The development of a School of Comparative Studies at Essex University, for example, subtly extends the emphasis on the experiential; the willingness within historical and literary studies in many places—notably East Anglia as well as Birmingham's Centre for Contemporary Cultural Studies— to come more nearly into the contemporary world, has something of the same consequence. The theological courses at Lancaster and Bristol incorporate the same principle. At the University of Ulster, the courses in West European Studies, Environmental Science, the History of Ideas and Modern International Migration, are among a number of attempts there to break down barriers between subjects while retaining intellectual content.

But in this group of universities as a whole there has still perhaps been rather less success at genuine interdisciplinary work than one might reasonably have hoped for. At East Anglia the pattern of degree courses, at any rate till recently, was such—as a commentator[1] has vigorously said—as 'to make it virtually impossible for the disciplines to remain in

1 Jenny Hughes, former editor of *Faculty*.

their tents; and yet to an amazing extent they seemed to have failed to come out of them . . . For preliminary courses in the School of Social Studies for example—economics, economic history, sociology and philosophy—are taught in very considerable isolation. Yet the connections which are there to be found cannot at that stage be discovered by the new student alone in his head.'

But it is unfair to mention particular universities when hardly any university in Britain, old or new, and no polytechnic either, has so far found the recipe for a course which shall be attractive, relevant, unified and truly interdisciplinary. Research on a considerable scale is needed to identify and comment upon the reasons both for the successes where they have occurred and the failures. How far is departmentalism the cause? To what extent is it the subject-confined courses which the teachers themselves took when they were undergraduates? How far is it their ambition for advancement in a world of specialised scholarship? How far is it the handicap caused by the narrow sixth form courses which the great majority of students will have taken during the two or three years before entry? How far does the fault lie with the structuring of various degree courses themselves? Do they make enough use of contacts with the outside world, and the 'teachable moments' which might be given when the students return from periods in a job, or from overseas, or from pursuing some investigation off campus? No one knows.

The predominant emphasis of the majority of the degree courses so far approved in Britain by the Council for National Academic Awards remains, of course, a professional one, within territories that are traditionally overseen by handsome guard dogs—of which the professional associations of engineers are splendid examples—trained to prowl their appropriate fields. Yet the broadening and humanising potential of the contact with the world which the sandwich principal gives to many C.N.A.A. courses is not to be underestimated, whether it takes a man for a year out of his polytechnic and into the world, or the student of social science out from the lecture room to meet the pain and conflict of life in the slums.

The Compendium of Degree Courses published annually by the C.N.A.A. shows year by year increasing numbers of authorised courses of a combined studies type leading to degrees awarded by the C.N.A.A. Some are promising—for example the modern studies course in history, politics and qualitative matters now offered at the Sheffield Polytechnic; those in humanities and in science and business studies, offered at the Thames Polytechnic; and that in science with industrial studies to be taken at Napier College in Edinburgh. None is in any profound sense interdisciplinary, but genuine efforts have been made to secure integration or interrelation between the subjects which are units within the whole. How far these courses are or will become or will stay integrated remains to be seen: one hopes that the extent of their success over the years will be reported on in due course as objectively as possible. It may be, in view of the history of developing institutions elsewhere, that in early days the enthusiasm and sense of purpose shared by so many members of staff will create a 'Hawthorne Effect', making viable enterprises which cease to be so when the mood changes. At that stage, it is possible that the lack of one powerful Head of a School of Combined or Interdisciplinary Studies may make itself destructively felt. Does any university or college take its undergraduate schools of interdisciplinary study seriously enough to appoint someone of professorial or equivalent rank to be their head? But how, even when this is done, can it be secured that he has sufficient confidence in himself, or in the mixture of disciplines he captains, to stand up against colleagues who are invulnerable because so armed with specialist knowledge?

In a number of ways the university most enthusiastic in following interdisciplinary concepts in structuring its courses, at least over the first two years, is the Open University. Its first year foundation courses are the products of team work. The first arts course aimed at making a survey of all the humanities in a general introduction, followed by a specific introduction to a number of separate subjects. There followed a series of chronological case studies, culminating in an eight-week case study of industrialisation and its impact on culture in Britain in the middle and later part of the nineteenth century. The foundation course in the social sciences, *Understanding Society*, posed the question 'Why do men live in societies?' which was taken up by each of the constituent disciplines in turn and followed by an examination in some detail of the population explosion today. The science foundation course included the subjects biology, physics, chemistry and the earth sciences, with a single pattern, the various laws of nature, providing the unifying theme (Stein, 1970, pp. 451-2). The scientists aimed 'to present and explain some of the concepts and principles of importance in modern science and to show how science, technology and society are inter-related'.

But though each course is interdisciplinary *within itself* there seems as yet to be little inter-faculty cross-fertilisation, and it may be that in the later years of his studies for a first degree the student will not at all necessarily be helped to develop a comprehensive outlook as much as he was in some earlier parts of the course. That remains to be seen.

What cannot be denied is that both in the United States and in Britain the curriculum in tertiary education for very many students remains narrow, eyes being fixed upon the attainment of specialist qualifications which will have professional and vocational value in the nearer future, including qualifications which enable their possessor to enter research. Pressures to go still further in this direction are very real, especially in the United States, the proliferation of departments and sub-sections of departments being often the danger sign. 'Fine arts may separate into art and music, earth sciences into geography and geology. English may spawn departments of linguistics and journalism, speech or psychology may form clinics . . . Irony lies in the fact that so many of the liberal arts professors themselves are not happy with genuinely liberalising and generalising courses. "For the most part", say the professors, "the courses are too introductory and elementary." Professors well versed in their fields prefer to teach the upper division and graduate courses, and these are specialised, applied and job-orientated. They are encouraged by the practice of placing a higher budgetary premium on services at the "upper" levels.' (Stein, 1970, pp. 451-2). Long-term considerations are clearly often being made subsidiary to short-term. Progress rather than civilisation is thought of as the ideal. Indeed it is naively assumed that the former will contribute automatically to the attainment of the latter. Much of the essential spadework, if successful collaboration between departments is to occur, remains to be done. This must include in some cases, as Daniel Bell (1966, pp. 283-4) has emphasised, the difficult task of searching out a conceptual language common to several fields. There is still no agreement between anthropologists and sociologists on the scope of the term 'culture'.

One of the most difficult problems of all in higher education is to encourage the direction of its evolution so that it reckons both with the desire of people to live in their own way (that is, have great freedom for personal development) and yet to find contributions which are deeply and personally satisfying to make to a society which itself has worthwhile purposes—a society in other words which exerts its authority upon the way in which its citizens will want to develop. The originating source for such worthwhile purposes must be the enlightened and disciplined insights of at least some of its inhabitants, past, present and future.

How far education at any level can help to solve such a problem must obviously be affected by the social temper. In a contemporary society no education will make much of a contribution unless at every stage, including that of higher education, it encourages and disciplines more than expertise —even if it is through the education of expertise that in the first place we must approach the broader and the more humane. 'What is needed', says David Edge, 'is to think of a way in which the achievement of knowledge can be regarded in much the same manner as the achievement of honesty, rather than as the scoring of goals.'[1]

Certainly no introduction of new types of course or new contents for existing courses will be successful unless they are felt to be necessary—that is to supply needs of which many people have *almost* become aware. The secret may be one of recognising such incipient awareness and hungers. If the maker of a syllabus, or a curriculum, simply inserts something new into the conventional pattern against the wishes or expectations of staff and students it is unlikely to be accepted, whether it be history for science specialists or chemistry for arts specialists or philosophy for either. As T. J. Grayson of the Centre for East European Studies at Birmingham University put it: 'If we try to introduce something, a foreign body, into our environment the environment will immediately reject it; whereas if the environment grows that thing within itself, it will not attempt to reject it. If we say that a remedy, a proper remedy, to one's narrowness is so and so the recipe will go in as a foreign body and the foreign body will be immediately rejected as the critical white corpuscles rush along and get rid of it.'

No doubt one must wait a little longer before the idea becomes common in the west that a period of higher education should train not only the capacity to be neutral but develop intelligent commitment. What we have normally been asking for in the communication of bodies of knowledge and a repertoire of physical or intellectual skills is neutral activity that is often a somewhat external acquisition. It may be that living in an industrialised, complicated world, in which mechanisms have so constantly to be attended to, tends to encourage people to concentrate on the outsides of things: to keep the mechanism running, to diagnose and cure faults as they arise, demands little feeling into situations, much detached analysis. Detachment is the modern virtue, imagination is seen only as an instrumental means to an end—and usually a quite short-term end.

It is difficult in the kinds of higher education we have

1 In a private communication to the author.

legitimised to find much place for the exercise of imagination of other than an instrumental kind, or for the growth of commitments—all of them subject to the criticism of the examining intelligence at every stage, but regarded as desirable, indeed indispensable, to the development of full maturity. The meagreness of the recognition given to the non-cognitive in higher education may itself be a factor in producing intelligent analyses of situations which are at the same time imperceptive because reckoning too exclusively with the intellectual elements in them. The habit is a common one among civil servants and sociological research workers but also among many other diagnosticians. The intellectual tends to turn people's lives into a succession of problems in order to deal with them: experiences are treated as if they were discardable; the significance of love and suffering and death as irrelevant. It may be that courses in higher education—whether they are specialist or not—will only be *effectively* interdisciplinary in their content if they can incorporate some elements that exercise modes of understanding in addition to the purely intellectual or cognitive.

The humanities ought to find it easier to do this than some other subject areas. Perhaps they have lost their way. What is their contribution to be in the 1970s and 1980s? Can they put men more nearly into touch with what they would really want if they knew what they wanted? Can a new concept of what the study of man means help the university to find its own *raison d'être* among the multiversities we have now?

Chapter 9

The Uses of the Humanities

I

Are universities simply to cater for the demands of the professions and of industry in contemporary society, or can they not give more leadership to that society, encouraging a greater proportion of their students to contribute thought and mind to its development? It is the failure of universities to do this that have made many critical of them. Cannot literature, philosophy, music and the arts, an imaginative understanding of history and theology, a humane psychology and anthropology, transform themselves into subjects which could further this aim? After all, the matter they are concerned with is man himself. To study them, it might be supposed, involves a reckoning with human nature and an awareness of the insufficiency by itself of all the knowledge which can merely be codified or talked about. But the humanities do not seem to have been helping as much as they might. Why not?

For one thing, they have been suffering from a feeling of inferiority in university circles. Even measured in such gross terms as the amount of financial support available to them, of research grants, of proportion of graduate students, staffing ratio, they come towards the bottom of the list. It is significant that while there are in Britain a Science Research Council, Medical and Agricultural Research Councils and a Social Science Research Council, a Humanities Research Council does not exist. In the United States, while there is now a National Endowment for the Humanities, its annual income, though recently increased, is a twentieth of that of the National Science Foundation. The feeling which the humanities have had of being somewhat disregarded has bred an inferiority complex in them which shows itself in a number of subtle ways that they might themselves indignantly deny. But it does take some explaining why in England the proportion of first class honours degrees should be so much lower in, say, English or history or theology, than in, say, chemistry or physics or botany. It is certainly not that their students enter with lower academic qualifications from school. The opposite is the case. Nor is there evidence to suggest that they are worse taught. Yet in most British universities over many years the proportion of firsts in humanities subjects has been not slightly but remarkably less than in science subjects.

Another possible manifestation of a feeling of inferiority is the conservatism of arts departments, on average, as compared with science departments, on average. Though there have been conspicuous exceptions, it is technology and science, rather than arts, departments which have more commonly shown themselves willing to adopt new forms of test and methods of examining, employ new teaching methods and so on. In universities offering courses in new methods of teaching to lecturers and professors in various subject areas— the courses largely being staffed by experts from those areas themselves— the demand has come from the medicals, engineers, pure scientists and lawyers, rather than from teachers of the humanities. This may or may not be a desirable form of conservatism, but conservatism it certainly is.

In the research field, it is very clear that the humanities for generations now have preferred their graduate students to take subjects that are 'tight' so that the findings can be tested by reference to texts and hard evidence. After all, it is argued, this is fairer to the candidate; it also makes the task of the examiners less impossible. But the consequent tendency, of course, is to make the subjects for Ph.D. researches in arts fields very limited in range and type. The following are thinly disguised actual examples: the development of stage-craft in

England, 1593-1603; a stylistic analysis of the sermons of William Hervey; techniques in the presentation of character in the early novels of D. H. Lawrence; the dating of the phases of the Battle of the Marne; a study of the linguistic features of the *Ancrene Riwle* (lines 30-41).

Work for a Ph.D. in any or all such subjects can be excellent in the intellectual discipline it provides, the exercise it gives to the will of the student and the training in the scholarship the subjects offer. But it can also enable him to conceal his personal tastes and judgements, even to discourage him from having any. And as time goes on the almost inevitable tendency will be for the subjects chosen in many arts fields to become less and less important, more and more confined and dealing with 'minute particulars'. Many indeed already lend themselves to the charge of being simply parts of an indiscriminate campaign to advance knowledge.

Much sociology and psychology still carry within their research methodology the suggestion that there was little essential difference between the study of things and the study of people. For certain purposes this no doubt is true. 'Behavioural science' has its uses, even as terminology, if we remember that human beings are capable of much more than merely behaving. One task of the humanities is surely to save people from assuming that love and kindness and suffering and imagining and dying are all just behaving. But so often the humanities, as taught, do little to rescue those who study them from such a *pis aller*. Students can even be diverted into looking at great literary, artistic and historical works as of importance mainly in illustrating sociological trends. Instead of enriching their imaginative and moral sensibility such a treatment encourages the idea that morality is nothing but conformity to the fashions of the day. The notion that we can come to know civilisation through impersonal study is a very common one, as is the idea that great books can survive summary or paraphrase into something that is not literature at all. Such notions are not innocent: they are sources of de-humanisation.

There is little doubt that it is easier to set examination questions which test finite knowledge—of facts or trends—rather than insight. And measurable goals are apt to affect our practice unduly, in part just because they are measurable. Fairness in examining calls for syllabuses that can be examined objectively, from the entrance stage to that of first degree. Publicised, tabular analyses of the numbers of first class honours degrees obtained, or records of Ph.D.s on the staff, or lists circulated around the university or polytechnic showing department by department the numbers of published papers during the year—all have their competitive value and no doubt act as incentives to many people to work and work hard But they have their dangers.

Liam Hudson (1972) has attacked with no mincing of words the simplistic image of man which much modern psychology projects. The professor of psychology or sociology, he contends, may advise his research students to stick to the hard facts: age, sex, social class, educational achievement, marriage and divorce rates, fertility, the incidence of disease and crime, rental values and what have you. 'The argument is beguiling and I succumb to it several times a year. But it remains chimerical. There is a profound pleasure to be had in hitching interpretations to data such as these. They form our anchor in times of need. But, in isolation, they are meaningless; and we tend, in any case, to absorb ourselves in playing statistical tunes upon them. Worse, if we are not scrupulous, we find ourselves edging round to the view that such simple facts are in some important sense basic; that people are reducible to the forms of evidence about them that we find it easiest to collect. The first, statistical, tendency is a form of scholasticism to which we are all subject in greater or lesser degree. The second, reductive, one is ideology, crude and brazen' (p. 155).

When it has been shown that a rat can learn a maze almost as well as a human being, says A. H. Maslow (1954), 'the maze should have been dropped once for all as an instrument for the study of learning. We know in advance that the human being learns better than the rat. Any technique than cannot demonstrate this is like measuring people who are bent over in a room with a low ceiling. What we are measuring is the ceiling, not the people. All that a maze does is to measure a low ceiling and not the height to which learning and thinking may go, not even in the rat. . . . How do people learn to be wise, mature, kind, to have good taste? To learn from tragedy, marriage, having children, falling in love? The learning of the heart has been neglected' (p. 372).

In too much research in the humanities, the devoted, clever candidate can take refuge from involvement and even from expressing any personal opinion at all by hiding himself, with the help of his statistical knowledge, behind a tabular or graphical statement compiled with great application and accuracy. But the test of a good historian is not only that he should have prised out everything that is to be found from the records, but also that he should continue to be able to feel something of the sweep of history, the power of personality, the relentlessness of events, the fighting for great causes that has gone on, so that victory has not been the tiny outcome of a tiny expediency, the sort of expediency which may be only too necessary if one is really to capture that Ph.D. It is obvious that scientists are reluctant to ask questions involving value-judgements. But so are most other specialists. For value questions can only be answered from outside their specialism (cf. Weinberg, 1968-69). The approach in contemporary works of scholarship to people in history or literature is too often a highly skilful attempt to take them to pieces and categorise the bits, without ever really putting them together again. The fact is that we do not in our researches in fields of the humanities often get deeply enough into essentials. We busily concentrate on externals.

With this withdrawal from the fight, the role of the humanities may become more and more one of subservience to the technologies. The majority of men in a mass society find entertainment and release in television and the film, in the theatre and books. The purpose of the arts and humanities is taken by very many to be not to lead anyone further into the meaning of things but rather to cajole us into acquiescing in a world where questions of meaning can have no meaning. And the humanities in the universities can easily become without realising it simply handmaidens in the task—with financial help from the powers that be to further its accomplishment.

When seminars of humanistic scholars are held, many of the best show themselves well aware of some of these dangers, and of others too. But their attitude frequently, in spite of the insights and imaginativeness they so often reveal, is one of puzzlement about what more direct or active contribution they or their subject might possibly make to society today, or in future. 'Let us', they are apt to argue, 'do what we can to make our students genuinely knowledgeable and thoughtful in the subject area which is our concern—with mastery, if that is possible for them, over one part of it. In this way they acquire something of the discipline of mind we would like them to have, and then we shall have given them something, at least, that is worthwhile, even though admittedly civilisation itself seems to be advancing in a direction we do not approve. But as teachers, or human beings even, we do not wish to involve ourselves too much in the fray.' This attitude deserved the tart comment it got from an observer at a recent conference which had gathered to discuss the function of humanistic studies in the 1970s: 'Others apart sate on a hill retir'd'.

Is it possible for the humanities to offer some alternative contribution which is more powerful and compelling? This might involve their going over to the offensive, and there are certainly risks in doing so. But going over to the offensive might compel them to face more of the facts: in these days the scientist, the social scientist and the applied scientist are all asking for help from the humanities.

Barnaby Keeney, formerly Chairman of the National Endowment for the Humanities in Washington, has suggested that in his view one way in which the humanities could make themselves useful would be by trying to throw new light on major contemporary problems. He gives as an example the work done by the late David Potter, Professor of History at Stanford, an expert on the period of the Civil War. He became interested in the refusal to accept a utilitarian ethic, a phenomenon familiar in present-day society, and was before his untimely death beginning to produce material which was highly relevant for practical application. Work in Urban Studies and Latin American Studies, properly done, must, Keeney points out, involve departments of history, government and economics. Basic knowledge, geographical, historical, cultural, about foreign territories which would be of great use to countries in studying issues of foreign policy almost certainly exists in the universities of the country concerned. Usually there is no means of filtering it through at the times when it might be most urgently needed in the process of decision.

But Keeney agrees that the greatest contribution the humanities could make would be to clarify the pattern of our value system. He is somewhat vague about how this might be accomplished, but suggests the formation of disciplinary and interdisciplinary groups from 'all appropriate disciplines in the humanities and social studies, to investigate and ascertain, if possible, the basis of contemporary society and the mandates of the contemporary environment and the consequences, so that from this knowledge may emerge precepts that are acceptable . . . to guide and hold the society together. We have in effect a choice between waiting for new values to emerge through evolution or to attempt to determine them. If this is done, they can be taught not didactically but through joint inquiry'.[1]

It seems reasonably clear that humanistic studies might be of use in helping policy decisions of many types: historical, social and literary studies may well inform us and make us more aware regarding many issues. I am not convinced, however, that such a contribution, important though it could

1 From a paper circulated privately in February 1972 and quoted with permission.

be, is the central one they need to make; or the one most distinctive of what I understand by the humanities. We no doubt need to make our present health and welfare services work more efficiently; to make our cities more planned and pleasant; the foreign policy of every country better informed. But the objectives of education through the humanities are not primarily useful even though we may harness them for use. There is little evidence that making the humanities more serviceable would civilise men more.

It is in fact sheer escapism to think that if we ensure that in some of their parts college and university courses address themselves to a number of the vital social issues of the day, we shall have done enough to humanise our students. This does not go to the root of the matter. It does not allow for the space and depth of soil men need for growth. There are many parts of human life to which 'decision-making' only applies in the very sense in which it would be misleading to use the term. The very popularity of the idea of educating the ability to make decisions, as if it were a capacity in itself, is testimony both to the superficiality of much contemporary educational theory and its excessive intellectualism. It is by no means clear that one can for instance *decide* to love or trust another human being.

How can one work out a humanistic curriculum which attends to social, even to behavioural, problems and yet offers a chance for contemplation too? The problem is to develop kinds of tertiary education which will produce people who have a disciplined grasp of an area of subject matter in depth, an educated awareness of social problems and also a personal sense of meaning and purpose. We have not as yet succeeded in attaining any of these objectives with enough students, but by and large we have succeeded better with the first than with the second and better with either than with the third. At this time is is particularly necessary to attend to this last: indeed continued success with the first two must depend upon doing this. However much one may be able to do in teaching subjects at the tertiary stage so as to link them with others and also, at least in some cases, to make their social relevance clear, it is difficult through most of them to exercise feeling and imagination in a personal way. To attempt to teach geography, or economics, or chemistry, for example, with such an objective in mind will almost certainly mean that at any rate in part they are being taught sentimentally and badly.

In teaching the humanities and the arts it is necessary to arouse both the emotions and the disciplined intelligence. This will usually arise through a sharing in feelings which are given expression in an ordered way—in music, for example, or in literature—and then actively reflected upon. Few students, whether their specialism is science, surgery, classics, engineering, housecraft, are incapable of moments of feeling of this mediated kind. But they need help—normally through example—if they are to express them or make use of them reflectively or even to recollect them in tranquillity.

Much has been written on the function of language in recording experiences. What is clear is that its function is not merely that of noting that the experience happened at such and such a time in such and such a place. Such a record would be that only of a diarist. Whenever we attempt to recollect an experience or reproduce it for ourselves or others in words or music or paint we are doing much more than copying. As Ernst Cassirer has said (1961), 'Those are mistaken for whom knowledge is nothing more than a simple corroboration of what is immediately given to us in elements of sense perception . . . Language is never a simple copy of contents and relations . . . (It) is a determinate and fundamental tendency of the mind's activity . . . and it is in these acts that a new aspect of reality—the actuality of things—first discloses itself to us' (p. 59).

It may be that a very important part of the education we can give anybody is encouraging him to express the experiences he has had *as experiences*, and that this is a distinctive part of the educative function of the humanities and the arts. In doing so he may enable himself to perceive more of their meaning. This may seem a very unrealist way of talking when we are confronted with a tongue-tied scholar, or the self-disciplined, self-denying research scientist. But he too as a man lives a life outside the laboratory or study; if he reads novels, sees films, listens to music, as he probably does, he may find in what they are saying elements which echo and extend his own experiences, tying them in to his life and giving it more meaning. Such reading, listening or seeing must involve an element of self-giving and imagination if they are to yield this product. To teach any subject well involves an appeal both to imagination and thought. The facts conveyed by the senses and by measurement in scientific observation are raw material; and the hypotheses and theories constructed to bring coherence to them are the outcome of imaginative effort. But in the arts as distinct from the sciences a personal participation is involved, what Max Black has called an 'empathic communion', so that we come to know a situation or an action from the inside.

I have earlier criticised the conventional concept of what are proper research subjects for Ph.D. purposes. This is not because I would wish to rule out subjects of the kind illustrated: they have and should have their place. But so also should subjects broader in scope. Sir Eric Ashby once described the touchstone of university studies as 'not to teach great truths but rather to teach truths in a great way'. The university's style of thought 'cannot be acquired except from someone who is constantly exploring at the limits of understanding (hence the necessity for academics to do what is commonly, and erroneously, called "research")'.[1] It is such an exploration at the limits of understanding which we need to encourage more of our advanced students to undertake; and here may be one of the avenues of most promise open to us. The demand from them should be for a thoughtful grappling with problems— philosophic, mathematical, scientific, political, moral, religious—which involves wide and deep reading (maybe in several languages) and a more personal contribution as well— certainly more personal than is usually asked for.

1 *Center Diary:* No. 14, 1966, p. 10. (Center for the Study of Democratic Institutions, Santa Barbara, U.S.A.)

It may be that today an approach to literature—potentially one of the most personal of subjects one can study—with first-year students in community colleges, polytechnics, many departments in universities themselves, should, as is done in a number of places, 'start where they are', that is, with attention seriously paid to the authors they are reading by choice in their leisure hours, even if of poor and evanescent quality. Another example of 'contemporary cultural studies' which might have point, at undergraduate as well as graduate level, is the programme conducted by Richard Hoggart and Stuart Hall at the University of Birmingham.

But, as Hoggart would not deny, there are dangers in an approach to the study of the humanities through contemporary events and contemporary literature unless the 'stuff of experience' in them can be used contemplatively and critically, involving many layers of the mind of the person who is watching or reading. Neither can the humanities assume that there exists only an 'eternal present' in which sensibilities are awakened anew as they are encountered; without an historical reference, a sense of the past, the humanities themselves may be only a myth and a commentary (cf. Bell, 1966, p. 283). How *much* meaning did that T.V. programme, that film, that novel, that newspaper account of a happening, really have? A student needs to develop a capacity to reflect in the round upon events that have come in upon him if he is to be educated by them. Television programmes, even of news, which retail the important and the unimportant in indiscriminate sequence; advertising; the pictures and reportage common in daily newspapers which encourage hardboiledness in the reader in sheer self-protection; the tendency everywhere to rob experiences of their leisure and depth and so allow them to spring back into mere events, encourages the external reception of life. The decline of religion as a medium for the expression of profound and personal feelings about life and death can also be a handicap. But of the stronger emphasis on the experiential now made by the young, and having its effects both inside and outside higher education, there can be little doubt. The 'relevance' for which there has been such a demand must include efficient communication of material and an education that is efficiently professional or vocational, for these conditions must be satisfied if the way is to be opened for other hungers to be appropriately appeased—whether the need is to care for, and be cared for by, others or to discover meaning in life by intelligent, personal exploration—but the relevance will be disastrously incomplete if that way is not then opened. To 'touch the top of a student's head and never his heart and senses' will not be enough; neither, however, will be an appeal to the heart and senses that bypasses the head.

II

The humanities, as we have suggested, are to be distinguished from the sciences by having as their main interest not groups or classes of things, but things in their uniqueness. Their prime concern is what happens or has happened to people as individuals or as members of society, not with deducing laws or theories from those happenings. They face life with all its rocks and its surprises; only after that is it their concern to speculate about the human condition or ameliorate it. Their first aim is to convey experience neat. Only when experiences have been achieved can they be evaluated. But though evaluation is indispensable, literature, the arts, architecture, religion, history, must start their work upon us by adding to our experience. They are not to be judged simply by their usefulness and there is danger in closing down too early upon an incoming experience in order to judge its worth. The openness or 'relaxation' of mind to which Wordsworth attached such great significance is a condition to which modern men—academics, scholars, scientists and technologists included—are tempted to give too little scope. And this is not merely a superficial openness. We may have to seek what we would prefer to shun. Tragedy is not a 'happiness'; but no education through the arts or the humanities is possible without discovery and a facing of the truths that we discover.

It is possible that some of the passion for good music, both classical and jazz, which is a mark of so many of the below-thirty age group in the west today, is that in such music men are to be heard speaking experientially and yet in an ordered fashion. There is no escape from truth—or reason—in seeing human beings so as to paint them as Rembrandt did, realistically. Who could possibly have imagined a dog or a sheep unless he has seen one? To perceive them and face the fact that they are *there* is 'reasonable': no logic or argument is involved. So also would the facing of many mysteries, including those of beauty, love and death. We demean and castrate them by translating them into 'problems'. One of the tasks of education—and to be continued through the tertiary stage—is to help people to recognise their own moments of insight. The process demands an ability to be passive, to wait, even to suffer. Otherwise we shall overlay these moments or prevent them arising at all.

If experiences are to educate us we must incorporate them—with as little loss as possible of their experiential force—according to an adequate pattern of coherence or evaluation or rationality. The unwillingness to allow that here is one of the great sources of the real contribution which the humanities can make to higher education, is shown in our very avoidance of words which emphasise a 'softer', 'feeling', attitude as compared with a 'harder' cognitive one. Thus 'compassion' is permissible in scholarly reference, but hardly 'love'; 'policies' are discussable, 'purposes' less so; we make 'models' rather than 'plans'; 'decision-making' is splendid, 'making good judgements' apparently not so crisp and exact and therefore not quite so praiseworthy, though the phrase is capable of much more content. But both feelings and reasoned judgements are necessary: it is as rational and essential to recognise, identify and incorporate feelings as it is to recognise and attend to facts. Feelings also bring knowledge. Knowledge from either source has its appropriate authority. To limit its source to what can be measured or proved is indeed to perpetuate, if not increase, the impoverishment of the authority of reason itself.

Knowledge, perhaps all knowledge, yields authority along two different lines. There is the objective authority yielded by experimentation. A scientific experiment can be repeated a thousand times and you will always get the same results if you do it properly. It is authoritative in that the outcome will be so and so and that the outcome will be the same each time and therefore it is truth that is being objectively demonstrated. Aesthetic or religious or moral truths cannot be demonstrated in the same way. In an appreciation of *King Lear* the key moment of insight may be the moment when we accept that man is indeed a poor, bare, forked animal. That is a rational act: but it is an act of perception rather than of proof. But the authority of such perceptions depends upon a consensus of personal insights. Such a consensus will always tend to be fragile and to depend upon the quality of the people who have had them.

It is certainly easy for the life of the feelings to be arrested at an adolescent stage, nor has much research been done even into what are the norms for emotional, aesthetic, religious or moral development. But the food for the imagination which the humanities can give is likely to nourish only if the surrounding climate is propitious. 'It is no such common matter', said Matthew Arnold, in a well-known passage at the end of his essay *The Function of Criticism*, 'for a gifted nature to come into possession of a current of true and living ideas and to produce amidst the inspiration of them.' But favourable currents and climates are needed for less gifted natures if they are to produce not perhaps books or scientific ideas but right judgements, sensitive discernments, imaginative understanding in their everyday lives and relationships. And it is, I maintain, the duty of a university to provide such a current of ideas, not only in a world of experimenters, but of those—including of course the experimenters themselves—who are also experiencers.

If the humanities are to have the educational impact they could have, their mediators will need to be people to whom their subjects matter both as experience and as a result of the subsequent reflection which intimately depends upon the experience itself. Denys Harding has described the influences on him at Cambridge of teachers 'who seemed to be living in their subject, not just lecturing in it'—as differentiated from teachers who 'might be well-read scholars, competent lecturers and some of them very kind as people. But they were looking at their subject from a safe and reasonable distance . . . From Leavis, Forbes and Richards one got the sense of people who were still struggling with problems in their subject and developing, who believed that every question should be met but who had for many of them no ready-packaged answer. The effect was to suggest that there were very high standards to be reached, beyond even these people who were so far beyond me'.[1]

For the teacher of the humanities to be successful in giving his students the necessary confidence in their own insights and power to judge their value, he will often need to care more and to be in closer touch with them than has of recent years been fashionable. At any rate some personal *rapport* between teacher and taught may often be helpful. Such *rapport* may require a greater degree of revelation of a teacher's own personal judgements and personal values than is usual, or indeed was necessary in an age where traditional norms of value were widely acceptable and actively believed in. All this calls for a certain kind of boldness in the university teacher; a degree of risk in showing his hand and contributing to a tradition of judgements, whether imaginative, aesthetic, or moral. But it will call for self-discipline too: he will not be out to convert his students to his own view-point or to sharing his own convictions. He will not be a proselytiser, or approach literature or art or history as if it had some specific 'message for today'. An objectivity will remain even in the lively contribution he makes and in his sharing of his experiences. His business is not to evoke feelings as ends in themselves. His business is rather to help his students to build up their own tradition of judgements that stem from personal and

1 In a paper read (1971) to a University of London Seminar on the Humanities. Quoted with permission.

felt experience and are to be incorporated into a rational sequence.

As Denys Harding goes on to say: 'In claiming for the humanities special responsibility for observing, sifting, comparing, considering human values I am not in the least tempted to suppose that they are therefore committed to the advocacy of particular policies when complex social and practical problems arise. Least of all must it be thought that a concern with humane values means introducing soft-heartedness into every problem in order to counteract the technologist's hard realism. The sensitiveness to the complexity and subtlety of human problems and human relations which the humanities develop is at the same time a form of severe realism, as a consideration of tragedy will suggest; it will not *simply* reinforce the fierce tenderheartedness of people who are crusading for this or that suffering section of our community. Faced for instance as we are with appalling ecological problems of overpopulation and a devastated habitat we shall not expect to find all the students of the humanities agreed on a policy; but the scientists, technologists and administrators who propose policies have eventually to argue them out within a perspective of values which has been established largely by work in the arts and the humanities in past generations and is constantly being modified by contemporary work of the same kind'.

The avoidance by scholars of large areas they regard, maybe subconsciously, as 'unsafe' is admirably shown by the choice psychologists make of subjects for research. They prefer tough-minded subjects rather than tender-minded ones. They conduct scores of investigations on aggression for every one on love. They study stress but not relaxation; pain but not delight; deprivation but not fulfilment; prejudice but not friendship (cf. Allport, 1963, p. 75). Perhaps the dangers of personal involvement are less if one studies the negative rather than the positive; one can escape further from any appearance of emotion or of having commitments and it is easier to remain in this way academically respectable.

Among the most dangerous of all humanities subjects is

theology or, as it is now coming to be called, religious studies. Safety and 'objectivity' can be obtained by making the curriculum in such fields almost entirely a study of Biblical texts, with much time naturally spent on mastering sufficient Greek and Hebrew, or the history of the early Christian Church and its doctrines, or religions other than Christianity. They are all highly desirable occupations, no doubt, but the study of religion must surely involve a feeling element, when man in his littleness is confronted with the immensities of the universe, the inevitability of death, the power of natural cataclysm. With no personal experiences of awe the student goes unaware of what has given rise to religions or religious belief. But in the conduct of many a theology department this can remain so tacit that it is never referred to. Worship may of course be examined sociologically or statistically as a phenomenon, but the feeling elements in it tend not to be regarded as academically relevant. An intelligent but remote, awe-proof, atheist could score on almost every examination paper as good a set of marks as an intelligent, religiously aware Moslem, Buddhist or Christian.

Enough has perhaps been said about the need for the humanities in higher education to be bolder in being human. The problem is not only one of incorporating such boldness in courses meant for those who are primarily students of the humanities, but of ensuring that some of their essential juices will nourish others whose main concern may be the technologies, law, science or medicine. And this can be extraordinarily difficult to do when the whole orientation of their courses may have encouraged a clinical approach and the assumption that inwardness and feeling have nothing to do with education. Away from the classroom and laboratory the young technologists may be readers of novels, worshippers in churches, keen upon nature, above all interested in people—and with considerable understanding of them. None of these, however, gets linked with what he or his teachers conceive as higher education.

Possible helps in this situation are, as we suggested in

Chapter 7, of three kinds. First, making freely available on or near the campus, and with the obvious backing of the institution itself, as many incentives as possible which encourage a more capacious and intelligent cultural life than the subject instruction embodies: large libraries, with open access; endowed concerts; the availability of video tapes and watching facilities for T.V. programmes of quality. This is hit-or-miss provision and has only sometimes been successful in the past. The libraries of most polytechnics and quite a number of technological universities are still starved of books even within specialist fields, let alone general ones; and a continuing starvation in the more general fields is almost guaranteed by prevalent concepts of 'cost benefit'. Second, the provision through counsellors, seminar and tutorial groups, the meetings of societies, and public lectures of stimuli to greater awareness of the tacit, 'feeling', sense knowledge of the world which all men possess and which makes meaning possible. The year in a sandwich course spent away from the university, polytechnic, or college may sometimes yield experiences of much more than a professional or industrial kind which can be fertilising. Third, and most practicable, the taking by teachers, of whatever subject, of opportunities to indicate some of their own wider and deeper concerns; their consciousness, that is, of a wider range of human problems than their subject by itself may immediately be about.

One problem in using the humanities in education in the way I have been suggesting is that of assessing what has been learned at the more profound levels in humanities 'subjects'. The students who simply let their emotions run sentimentally away with them should certainly be marked down; but those whose judgements reveal no sign of their having 'been inside' a piece of literature or any of the historical, anthropological or psychological situations they are describing, should be marked down too. Evidence of genuine understanding, imagination and reflection is what we are looking for. Neutrality pursued as an end in itself is not enough; the disciplined balance which can follow the acts of feeling and perception is a very different thing.

The choice before the humanities is clear; either to pretend to be sciences or to acknowledge without shame the experiencing and imaginative elements within any essential study of them. Four of the questions of most concern to our time are: What is the place of value in a world of facts? How can sensibility nourish thinking with neither element denuded? How is belief, religious and moral, to be related to the denial of belief? Can anyone belong to the future without inheriting the past and the present? *Le passé n'est pas passé.* Only by breathing the climate in which such battles are to be waged can anyone get a really adequate higher education. No institution in which such warfare is not going on is really a university or a *poly*technic.

A place of higher education which is to matter much to its students—or to its country—must be one through which the mental impulsions of the time flow and in which battles of ideas are being fought out. This makes for tensions; but without such tensions the thinking done in the university or the polytechnics will be of relatively minor import and the teaching it is able to give will be lacking in power.

As far as the student is concerned, he needs to feel some of the conflicts within himself. He must see for himself that at every instant he too belongs to the past as well as the present and that it is fatal to belong only to one of them. He must realise that facts have no meaning without values and that innovations have no point without a worthwhile civilisation to which they contribute. How to bring such a state of mind to birth not merely in 200 students a year, but 200 000, is the problem. It will not be solved without a lot of courage on the part both of members of staff and of students; or without a great deal more attention being given to the range and the depth of the content of the higher education we offer the individual, nor without a lot more willingness on the part of one place of higher education to learn from another than most of them at present show.

Chapter 10

Universities Between Two Worlds

We have been suggesting that today universities are between two worlds both chronologically and ideologically. It remains to sum up and to deduce the consequences of the position taken.

The period 1950-70 saw a rapid enlargement of the world's population, with great strides taken in many countries in the development of society. People's expectations grew fast of what life had to offer them in opportunity and affluence. The period 1970-2000 is likely to see even more rapid changes. The population of the world still increases alarmingly and there is greater need than ever before for planning and the application of rigorous scientific thought. That combination is likely to yield far more leisure—or unemployment—for the majority of people, but it may well call for a smaller, not a larger, *proportion* of sheer experts highly trained in the universities of Europe and the United States. This for two reasons. First, with many more countries developing systems of higher education of their own, the extent of their dependence upon the products of the universities of other countries will be lessened, though it will still remain appreciable. Secondly, while the increased centralisation, mechanisation and sophistication of life may well stimulate the demand for limited numbers of inventors and administrators of high quality, who will compete for the jobs available, the demand for graduates with a rather lesser expertise, though a first class intelligence, may be reduced, if not in their absolute numbers at least in the percentage of the population involved. In other words the market for 'top' experts may be strong even in comparison with the present day; but we may find that the densely populated world is producing a superfluity of experts at other levels, even if each only works a fifteen- or twenty-hour week. In this situation should not many universities—and polytechnics and other institutions of higher education—contract in size or close down altogether?

By no means. But what will become more and more clear is that their main job is no longer that of producing technological experts. The period of their history in which that was taken for granted will be seen as transitional. The world into which mankind will be moving will be one needing more, not less, education, but an education which tries to cater for human development more directly. Of course universities must still train people who will be able to tackle the technical problems—for example the problem of feeding the vast extra number of mouths; of travelling faster and more often; of an urban world. If they trade out from doing this, they will not belong to the modern world any more and will certainly be replaced by institutions which are more useful.

But if universities drift into becoming places of multitudinous utility—without, it may be, altogether realising the fact—it will be only a matter of time before it becomes clear that this is reductionism and that their quality cannot be measured in terms of productivity alone. The personal and social progress which matters even more is in mental span, moral development, range of imaginative apprehension. People will need to be helped to develop further and more sensitively their powers of enjoyment, their sense of purpose, their capacity for empathy and moral action. And they will need to do this as individuals, not merely as imitators of others.

It used to be common for the élite members of a society to act as the transmitters of the moral code and upholders, at any rate publicly, of the view of the world or the religious faith which all the other members would be expected to adopt—

which they would indeed find it natural to adopt. Kings and leaders told their people what they should believe. 'Then King Darius wrote unto all people, nations and languages that dwell in all the earth: "Peace be multiplied unto you. I make a decree, that in every dominion of my kingdom men tremble and fear before the God of Daniel"' (Daniel VI, *vv*, 25-6). For most of the world's history so far, people could be experts technically—they could be carpenters, farmers, merchants, soldiers, scribes—and function efficiently and happily without any high degree of individualisation. One hardly needed to arrive at convictions that were individual on any deep matter: one simply and naturally adopted those of one's society. In clothes, manners, nationalism and patriotism, one followed the fashions of one's class or one's occupation. There might be different élites to respect for different sectors of one's life— princes who formed an élite, bishops and priests who formed an élite, doctors, lawyers, grandparents. The sources of most of the authority even over the mature man or woman were almost always outside him. He might be a master of his craft but morally he was an obedient servant. He was obedient to the rules given him from without, not dependent upon his own insights save in small degrees.

The general direction of the evolution of our society now, especially for its more intelligent members, is and must continue to be towards greater and greater individual aware- ness and self-dependence. The words élite and élitist have in our time acquired a sinister sound. One of the animating impulses for men in many countries is towards more equality. Nor will they be content for long if for prince and bishop are substituted big-businessman or clever scientist. These may well be respected as experts within their range of competence, as financial manipulators, ingenious inventors or whatever. But that is very different from their being regarded as authorities or guides on how life should be lived. It is no far step from this position to one in which universities and other places of higher education could come to be accepted within their range of competence as useful, even indispensable, service stations for the modern world—but as little or nothing more. We may ask their professors to see round more of the corners ahead than we can ourselves; we may ask universities to solve more complicated problems than we are capable of doing; and to be great reservoirs of knowledge and skill. But we hesitate to ask them to be places of reflection or thought except for specific and directed technological, scholarly or research enterprises.

The fact is, however, that maintenance of the trust of a people in those who have been highly educated, its powerful civil servants and its scientists for example, is dependent upon their having not only knowledge but vision too. The universities from which they come are expected to play their part in securing both. Society in spite of its hesitancies finds that it does need people—many of them in universities—to feed it with imaginative ideas, some of fundamental import. Through the years its own direction of development has been altered, by men whose ideas, whether or not they were themselves at a university, have been given effective currency by the missionary work of such places. In the past two hundred years these have included Kant, Goethe, Coleridge, Darwin, Marx, Kierkegaard, Nietzsche, Durkheim, Freud.

Any system of higher education is going in future to be more and more dependent both for its financing and for the degree of freedom given to it or to any of its parts upon the public's faith in it. This in some part certainly depends on the recognition by people of its usefulness, but it depends too on their recognition, whether overt or covert, that it stands for values less immediate and definable than use. Even public readiness to respect research has within it an ingredient or two other than an anticipation of larger crops, more effective drugs, more ingenious weapons, better transport, however surely these are expected dividends. There is also a suspicion, however faint sometimes, that to know the truth is important, whether it be in our favour or not; that insight matters, as do knowledge, logic, justice and sense of purpose. Any institution which shows that it values these will, in a free country, be given a certain respect.

This is the basic justification for according a higher measure of academic freedom to institutions of higher education. Unless, however, they continue to deserve it and are widely felt to deserve it, they are always, and will always be, in danger of losing it.

An enlightened state, an enlightened local education authority, an enlightened religious denomination, may give an institution of higher education almost, if not quite, all the freedom it can use. But each may be tempted on occasion to say: 'It is imperative now for us to have people who will make themselves efficient instruments for national or industrial or denominational purposes: soldiers, machine minders, staunch defenders of given doctrines, who will obey the rational only as we see it'. In these circumstances it may be part of the mission of the university, and of other places of higher education also, to put such—it may be quite necessary—obedience into its temporary place while standing for, and proclaiming, the importance of both a wider imagination and a wider reason. For most purposes and for much of the time institutions of higher education may not need any more autonomy than they are allowed by those who sponsor them. But on occasion they may need, and should be able to come under, an umbrella which is the joint and conscious property of all those institutions. Because of the need in a community for thought, foresight and understanding, and the dangers that civilisation will be engulfed, a university cannot without betraying itself opt out of the situation.

A university, however, may not be willing to accept other institutions of higher education as companions under an umbrella, for another reason than a temptation to sit pretty to its social responsibilities. It may, as we have seen, have too limited a concept of the nature of rationality and of ways of attaining it and regard quite a number of subjects of study which are pursued in other institutions of higher education as too unintellectual for recognition. The adjective 'rigorous'— an excellent word in its place—can be used unreasonably to confine the territory of reason itself. How far should a university ever have to hear about, let alone seriously consider as studies, such subjects as drama, creative music, social work, sculpture, housecraft, physiotherapy? It should, even if it is at the apex of the hierarchy, certainly *care* about them. It is bad in almost every way for universities to be ivory towers with impermeable walls. Such subjects need not be abhorrent if they too are studied in an environment where intelligence is respected and the dominant values are both evaluative and distinctively humane. The making of the syllabuses for such subjects and the teaching of courses in them should of course be in the hands of the relevant experts. As it is, applied subjects with a not necessarily much larger theoretical basis abound in both universities and polytechnics—from dairy farming to estate management, from concrete engineering to dentistry, from transportation studies to marketing.

A time of financial stringency such as the one we have now entered challenges our priorities robustly. The state may decide that higher education is both too important and too expensive to be left to the academics and it will interfere directly and vigorously. But systems planning and cost benefit analysis by themselves solve no moral question. A calculating rationalism is not capacious enough in its presuppositions about human nature. Nor is it any answer to what Alvin Toffler has recently called 'the quiescent but still simmering disaffection of youth'.

Most departments in institutions of higher education of all types want to modify presuppositions—though not always enough—as well as to impart facts and skills. Their teachers want students to acquire knowledge and to develop a capacity to examine evidence with detachment, but also to develop fairmindedness, tolerance, convictions and confidence in facing the world. Few teachers in polytechnics, or universities, at bottom want their students to be careerists in their orientation and nothing more.

In both kinds of institution they fail to make this sufficiently clear. If higher education—whether pursued in universities or polytechnics—is going to be able to help as it should to counter the drift and the tendency to dissolution of our time, its teachers need to be more in touch with themselves and with each other, and to face more unitedly the underlying task they have in common.

In the thinking about the content of higher education too small a part is being played by those who think from first principles, too large a part by the activists and planners. But what the former have to say, if it could be made forcefully articulate, could do much to compel us to go back to principles at a time when to do that is vital. Men—including the economists and planners—know at heart so much more than they say or even reckon with. And it is knowledge at this level that we need to draw upon.

To cater for national and personal needs adequately is, then, a job common to universities and polytechnics. Their students are equally human beings; and many in future will be having part of their higher education in one type of institution and part in another. If Britain has been rather disenchanted with its universities in the last half-dozen years, it could easily become just as disappointed with its polytechnics, towards the end of another half-dozen—especially if they produce only functionaries, however efficient, and not educated men and women.

No doubt polytechnics hope increasingly not to lay themselves open to this charge. University teachers and polytechnic teachers have a large measure of freedom to teach in the way they want, and, in considerable degree, what they want. The wanting, however, often lacks sufficient range and depth. Universities and polytechnics are not adequately mission-oriented, in social or in human terms. No one wants the polytechnics to imitate the universities. But that they will more and more be complementary parts of one higher education system needs emphasising. Underneath the necessary and desirable differences, they have civilising and moral objectives in common. Methods of attaining these call for much continuing joint discussion and a deeper understanding of what is involved.

Governments, as we said earlier, tend to pay institutions of higher education to produce experts of the sorts they judge they most need, experts who as technology advances tend to acquire more and more power to affect the daily lives of millions. It is particularly for the institutions who educate to degree level to produce graduates who have a necessary fear of the consequences of the exercise of their own power; and foresight enough to control those consequences, as far as may be, on behalf of us all. In the long run no doubt it is *this* achievement that governments will be willing to pay most for—in respect and even in hard cash; but if it is too long a run men may have lost much of their humanity *en route*, with few noticing that it has happened. The higher education system of any advanced country is certainly going to continue to comprise a diversity of institutions with overlapping functions. It is important that differences in immediate objective and of administrative control should not obscure their underlying community of purpose.

Throughout this book it is the importance of the personal education of the student that has been stressed: in reaching down to the sources of authority there is no possible substitute for insights that come individually if they are to come at all. Some of them will be insights into the absoluteness of the objectivity of fact, of 'the armies of unalterable law' which govern the behaviour of the universe as it is encountered or seen. Some will be insights less magisterial but more intimate.

Ben Jonson's *Timber* quotes a passage from the *Famosa Apologia* of the physician Mayerne—a passage from which incidentally the motto of the University of Lancaster is taken. 'Patet omnibus veritas,' it begins—'Truth lies open to all, it is not yet anyone's possession. Much of it is left even for those to come. Nothing is more hostile to truth than to take away freedom to speculate.' Yes, indeed, but only some *kinds* of truth will be yielded by an attitude of speculation, even in higher education. The direction in which men look will affect and limit what they are able to see. Truth may lie open to all, but only to the extent and from the directions that they lie open to receive it. Men are so often 'distraught by expectancy', to use Rilke's phrase, that it is only with difficulty that they will notice what they are not expecting, or almost expecting, to see. It follows, as I have implied in earlier chapters, that the education of the inward glance is of fundamental importance: it is this which affects the evidence we shall be able to recognise as authoritative or even be able to recognise as evidence at all.

Places of higher education need to widen the area of their search for truth. Unless they do they will lack the communication with some of the sources of authority essential to the giving of the leadership, and producing the kind of men, needed if the world is not to relapse into a new barbarism. Our reliance on technology cannot but increase; yet we are at the stage of having lost the faith that science in itself is good or its ethical neutrality really trustworthy. New contacts with the sources of illumination, and therefore of authority, are imperative.

In his *Mission of the University*, Ortega y Gasset (1946) declares in his typically emphatic way that the culture of the Middle Ages was a way of looking at things. It involved the system of ideas concerning the world and humanity which the man of that time possessed; it was a repertory of convictions which became the effective guide of his existence. 'Life is a chaos, a tangled and confused jungle in which man is lost. But his mind reacts against the sensation of bewilderment: he labours to find "roads", "ways" through the woods in the form of clear, firm ideas concerning the universe, positive convictions about the nature of things. The ensemble, or system, of these ideas, is culture in the true sense of the term; it is precisely the opposite of external ornament. Culture is what saves human life from being a mere disaster; it is what enables man to live a life which is something above meaningless tragedy or inward disgrace' (pp. 43-4).

Higher education, I believe, needs to develop new orientations. The answer on the part of the universities cannot be in their concentrating upon being multiversities alone; nor upon their withdrawing into a concentration on pure scholarship and research. They must remain places of personal and civilising education for an actual and living society. They need in other words to link the world of scholarship and research with that of action, to link the affective with the cognitive. They need to be both places of knowledge and places with spirit; in touch both with the objective and with the subjective. In such a linkage there is bound to be conflict. 'Is it the task of the university to be a clerisy, self-consciously guarding the past and seeking assertively to challenge the new? Or is it just a bazaar, offering Coleridge and Blake, Burckhardt and Nietzsche, Weber and Marx as antiphonal prophets, each with his own call? No consensual answer is possible, perhaps because the university is no longer the citadel of the traditional mode—only the simple-minded can believe it is—but an arena in which the critics once outside the Academy have, like the tiger (or Tyger) once outside the gates of society, found a place—deservedly—within. And the tension between past and future, mind and sensibility, tradition and experience, for all its strains and discomfitures, is the only source for maintaining the independence of inquiry itself' (Bell, 1966, p. 149).

At any one moment of time if the university is alive such tension, vitally held, may be perceived as present as strenuously as it is in one of the world's great bridges—the Maracaibo Lake Bridge in Venezuela, the Verrazano Suspension Bridge at the entrance to New York harbour, the Severn Bridge at the Beachley-Aust crossing; as it is in the pity and terror brought together in a great Greek or Elizabethan play; or in the straining sexual opposites united and evolvingly fulfilled in a great Mozartian duet like 'Là ci darem la mano' in *Don Giovanni*. The kind of knowledge the university has to convey is knowledge that is still alive, still leaving experiences behind it. It is in the experiencing afresh again and again that the educative power of knowledge rests. That word 'rests' is full of a calm activity.

To say that a place of higher education should produce an élite is to say among other things that it should produce more people who have access to their own experiences and can evaluate them. It is through such people that a direction of looking is mediated. We catch presuppositions and assumptions from people who hold them. But what is the range and scope of the personal involvement brought into the reckoning? Is the content of higher education to be limited to those kinds of knowledge and skill which will be contributed only by an observer who has learned to be detached and unmoved? Is 100 000 000 always to be $10^4 \times 10^4$ or sometimes to be ten thousand times ten thousand? Unless places of higher education in future serve mankind in more than clever but utilitarian ways they will deservedly if slowly come to forfeit confidence. For in spite of all our planning they will fail of real purpose, fail to bridge the gap between the world of the past and that of the future, between the world outside man and the world within him.

References

ALLPORT, GORDON (1963) 'Imagination in Psychology: Some Needed Steps', in *Imagination and the University*, The Gerstein Lectures, Ontario: York University.

BECKER, H. S., GEER, B. and HUGHES, E. C. (1968) *Making the Grade*, New York: John Wiley.

BELL, DANIEL (1966) *The Reforming of General Education*, New York and London: Columbia University Press.

BERNSTEIN, B. (1967) 'Open Schools, Open Society?', in *New Society*, No. 259, 14 September.

BETTELHEIM, BRUNO (1961) *The Informed Heart*, London: Thames and Hudson.

BRECHT, BERTHOLT (1960) *The Life of Galileo*, trans. Versey, D. I., London: Methuen.

BRIGGS, ASA (1964) 'Drawing a New Map of Learning', in Daiches, D. (ed.) *The Idea of a New University: An Experiment in Sussex*, London: André Deutsch.

BROTHERS, J. and HATCH, S. (1971) *Residence and Student Life*, London: Tavistock Publications.

CASSIRER, E. (1961) *The Logic of the Humanities*, trans. Howe, C. Smith, New Haven and London: Yale University Press.

CHICKERING, A. W. (1969) *Education and Identity*, San Francisco: Jossey-Bass

COOPER, IRVING S. (1969) 'Medicine of the Absurd', in Nash, Arnold S. (ed.) *The Choice Before the Humanities*, Durham, North Carolina: Regional Education Laboratory for the Carolinas and Virginia.

COUNCIL FOR NATIONAL ACADEMIC AWARDS (Annual) *Compendium of Degree Courses*, 3 Devonshire Street, London W1N 2BA.

DEARDEN, R. F., HIRST, P. H. and PETERS, R. S. (eds) (1972) *Education and the Development of Reason:* London and Boston: Routledge and Kegan Paul.

DRESSEL, P. L. and DELISLE, F. H. (1969) *Undergraduate Curriculum Trends*, Washington, D.C.: American Council on Education.

Early Development of the Open University, The (1972) Report of the Vice-Chancellor, January 1969—December 1970, Bletchley, Bucks.: The Open University.

Education and the Nature of Man (1967) Joint Study Commission on Education, (ed. K. Bliss): World Council of Churches.

ERIKSON, ERIK H. (1961) 'The Roots of Virtue', in Huxley, Julian (ed.) *The Humanist Frame*, London: George Allen and Unwin.

FELDMAN, K. A. and NEWCOMB, T. M. (1969) *The Impact of College on Students*, San Francisco: Jossey-Bass.

FRIEDENBERG, E. Z. (1969) 'Social Consequences of Educational Measurement', in *Proceedings of the 1969 Invitational Conference on Testing Problems*, Princeton, New Jersey: Educational Testing Service.

FRYE, NORTHROP (1969) 'The University and Personal Life: Student Anarchism and the Educational Contract', in Niblett, W. R. (ed.) *Higher Education: Demand and Response*, London: Tavistock Publications.

GOODLAD, J. S. R. (1973) *Science for Non-Scientists*, London: Oxford University Press.

HARVARD COMMITTEE REPORT (1946) *General Education in a Free Society*, Cambridge, Mass.: Harvard University Press.

Higher Education (1963) Report, Prime Minister's Committee (Robbins Report), London: H.M.S.O.

Higher Education Review (1972) Vol. 4, No. 3.

HIMMELWEIT, HILDE T., OPPENHEIM, A. N. and VINCE, P. (1958) *Television and the Child*, London: Nuffield Foundation, Oxford University Press.

HUDSON, LIAM (1972) *The Cult of the Fact*, London: Jonathan Cape.

JACOB, P. E. (1957) *Changing Values in College*, New York: Harper and Row.

JENCKS, C. and RIESMAN, D. (1968) *The Academic Revolution*, Garden City, New York: Doubleday and Co.

JENKINS, DANIEL (1966) *The Educated Society*, London: Faber and Faber.

KAYSEN, C. (1969) *The Higher Learning, the Universities and the Public*, Princeton, New Jersey: Princeton University Press.

KERR, CLARK (1963) *The Uses of the University*, Cambridge, Mass.: Harvard University Press.

MASLOW, A. H. (1954) *Motivation and Personality*, New York: Harper and Row.

MOBERLY, SIR WALTER (1949) *The Crisis in the University*, London: S.C.M. Press.

MORISON, R. S. (1964) 'Foundations and Universities', in *The Contemporary University; Daedalus*, Fall.

MORRIS, SIR CHARLES (1962) 'The Function of Universities Today', in Niblett, W. R. (ed.), *The Expanding University*, London: Faber and Faber.

MORRIS, COLIN (1972) *The Discovery of the Individual 1050–1200*, London: S.P.C.K.

MOUNTFORD, SIR JAMES (1972) *Keele: An Historical Critique*, London: Routledge and Kegan Paul.

NEWCOMB, T. M. and WILSON, E. K. (eds) (1966) *College Peer Groups*, Chicago: Aldine Publishing Co.

New Students and New Places (1971): A Report and Recommendations by the Carnegie Commission on Higher Education, New Jersey: McGraw Hill.

NIBLETT, W. R. (ed.) (in preparation) *The Sciences, the Humanities and the Technological Threat*, London: University of London Press.

ORTEGA Y GASSET, J. (1946) *Mission of the University*, London: Kegan Paul, Trench, Trubner and Co. Ltd.

PERKIN, H. J. (1969) *New Universities in the United Kingdom*, Paris: O.E.C.D., and London: H.M.S.O.

RIEFF, PHILIP (1966) *The Triumph of the Therapeutic*, London: Chatto and Windus.

RIKER, H. C. (1956) *Planning Functional College Housing*, New York: Teachers College, Columbia University.

ROSZAK, THEODORE (1972) *Where the Wasteland Ends*, Garden City, New York: Doubleday and Co.

SANFORD, NEVITT (ed.) (1962) *The American College*, New York and London: John Wiley.

SANFORD, NEVITT (1967) *Where Colleges Fail*, San Francisco: Jossey-Bass.

STEIN, JAY W. (1970) 'Administering Liberal-General Education for all Students', in *Journal of Higher Education*, **41**, *vi*, Ohio: Ohio State University Press.

STUDY COMMISSION ON UNIVERSITY GOVERNANCE REPORT (1968) *The Culture of the University: Governance and Education*, Berkeley, California: University of California.

TRILLING, LIONEL (1966) *Beyond Culture*, London: Secker and Warburg.

TROW, MARTIN, (1972) 'The Expansion and Transformation of Higher Education', in *International Review of Education*, **18**, *i*, Hamburg: Unesco Institute for Education.

UNIVERSITY GRANTS COMMITTEE (1957) Report on *Halls of Residence*, London: H.M.S.O.

UNIVERSITY GRANTS COMMITTEE (1967) *University Development 1962–1967*, London: H.M.S.O.

WEINBERG, A. M. (1968/69) 'Scientific Choice and the Scientific Muckrakers', in *Minerva*, **7**, *i–ii*.

WOODS, G. F. (1965) *Contemporary Theological Liberalism*, London: A. and C. Black.

Appendix

Members of Working Parties mentioned in the Preface:

Richard Andrews, R. A. Becher, Professor Seymour Betsky, Gerald Collier, Dr John Coulson, John Dancy, Dr W. Davey, the Rev. Dr A. O. Dyson, Dr David Edge, Professor John Ferguson, Dr Sinclair Goodlad, T. J. Grayson, Professor Denys Harding, Professor Barbara Hardy, John Heywood, Donald Hutchings, Professor L. C. Knights, Mrs Marion Milner, Professor Ben Morris, Professor Arnold Noach, Professor Richard Peters, Dr Stephen Prickett, Dr Marjorie Reeves, the Rev. Canon James Robertson, Professor Ninian Smart, Professor Stephen Spender, Dr Frances Stevens, Dr P. J. T. Tait, the Rev. Dr George Tolley, Professor Henry Walton, the Rev. George Whitfield.

Index